the **KING FAMILY** cookbook

The King Family Cookbook
© 2009 Xan Albright. All Rights Reserved.

All photos, illustrations and text are the personal property of members of The King Family.

No part of this book may be reproduced in any form or by any means, electronic, mechanical, digital, photocopying or recording, except for the inclusion in a review, without permission in writing from the publisher.

Published in the USA by:
BearManor Media
P O Box 71426
Albany, Georgia 31708
www.bearmanormedia.com

ISBN 1-59393-504-8

Printed in the United States of America.

Layout and cover design by
Rene Reyes and Shane Rosamonda/Polly O. Entertainment, LLC.

www.officialkingfamily.com

the
KING FAMILY
cookbook

275 Fun, Fabulous, New and Retro Recipes from
"America's First Family of Song"

Compiled & Edited by Xan Albright
with Erin Albright Arnett *and Tina Cole*

On the set of the family's 1967 television special
"Thanksgiving with the King Family"

CONTENTS

CONTRIBUTORS............................i

FAMILY TREE.............................ii

ABOUT THE KING FAMILY...................1

INTRODUCTION............................3

CELEBRATE WITH THE KING FAMILY..........9

MAIN DISHES............................13

SOUPS..................................73

SALADS & DRESSINGS.....................85

BRUNCHES & VEGETABLES.................113

DESSERTS..............................135

BEVERAGES, DIPS, SAUCES & APPETIZERS..201

BREADS................................221

RECIPE INDEX..........................235

Family & friends in January 2005 at Cam Clarke's party for Vonnie's 85th birthday and the 40th Anniversary of "The King Family Show"

Thank you to all our family's contributors:

Pearl Driggs

(the Mother, Grandmother and Great Grandmother of them all)

Karleton King Driggs and
  Cheryl Driggs (daughter-in-law)
  Ray Driggs (son)

Maxine King Thomas and
  Donna Thomas (daughter-in-law)
  Carolyn Cameron (daughter)
  Shauna Elliott (granddaughter)
  Wendy Moran (granddaughter)
  Amy Nottingham (granddaughter)
  Sarah Thomas (granddaughter)

Luise King Rey and
  Alvino Rey (husband)
  Carla Rey (daughter-in-law)
  Liza Butler (daughter)
  Chick Rey (daughter-in-law)
  Cherilyn Church (granddaughter)

Alyce King Clarke and
  Ric de Azevedo (son)
  Anna de Azevedo (daughter-in-law)
  Jennifer Suttner (granddaughter)

Donna King Conkling and
  Candy Brand (daughter)
  Jamie Miller (daughter)
  Chris Conkling (son)
  Xan Albright (daughter)
  Laurette Walton (daughter)
  Kristen Gurksnis (granddaughter)
  Brooke Smith (granddaughter)
  Noelle Sanderson (granddaughter)
  Kelly Miller (granddaughter)
  Lorie Albright (granddaughter)
  Erin Arnett (granddaughter)
  Annie Wilkins (granddaughter)
  Stefanie Heaton (granddaughter)

Yvonne "Vonnie" King Burch and
  Tina Cole (daughter)
  Cathy Green (daughter)

Phyllis Heim (widow of Bill Driggs) and
  Steve Driggs (son)
  Diana Driggs (daughter-in-law)
  Debbie Fox (daughter)
  Jani Driggs (daughter-in-law)

Marilyn King and
  Dale Foshée (son-in-law)
  Wendy Lloyd (daughter-in-law)

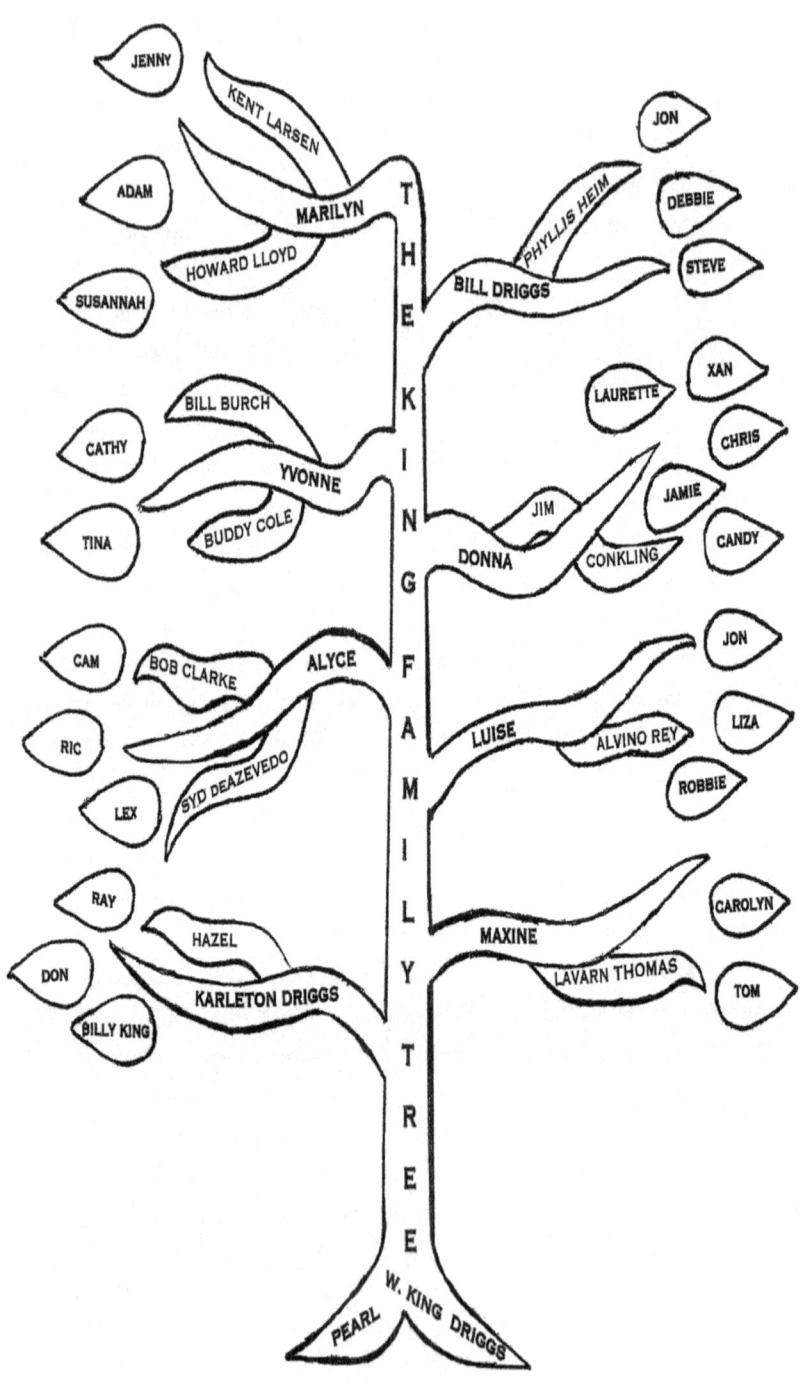

ABOUT THE KING FAMILY

Originally christened "America's First Family of Song," The King Family exploded onto the national entertainment scene in 1965. Centered around the popular talents and rich harmonies of Grammy® nominated Big Band era greats The King Sisters, along with bandleader and guitar virtuoso Alvino Rey, the entire family displayed on weekly national television the musical talents of its 37 members, spanning three generations. Following just two dazzling appearances on ABC-TV's "The Hollywood Palace," The King Family became one of the most popular and beloved television, recording and concert acts of the 1960's and 70's.

The King Sisters, a popular recording group with a unique 4-part harmony sound, began performing with the Horace Heidt Orchestra in the late 1930's. As they continued into the 40's and 50's with bandleader Artie Shaw, and eventually joining the Alvino Rey band, they became one of the leading attractions of the day on records, radio, movies and the concert stage.

As the King Sisters' own families expanded, the musical magic was eventually captured in 1965 in their own weekly ABC-TV show, featuring not only the King Sisters and Alvino Rey, but all the aunts, uncles, siblings, cousins, and little kiddies of 37 members. This initial TV series would spawn a show-business phenomenon that over the next decade would encompass 17 television specials, including holiday specials, 6 top-selling albums for Warner Bros., and a second TV series. During these years, the family's schedule also included record-breaking engagements at the nation's top concert venues including sold-out performances at The Hollywood Bowl, nightclub engagements in Las Vegas, Reno, and Lake Tahoe, appearances at Disneyland, and a "King Family Day" at the New York World's Fair.

The King Family continued to appear together in concert and on television throughout the 1970's and The King Sisters continued into the 1980's. In 1985 the Sisters were one of the featured performers at President Reagan's Inaugural Ball and in 2004, The King Family's unique place among the pantheon of entertainers associated with the holidays, including Andy Williams and Judy Garland, was celebrated as part of the BRAVO Television Network's documentary "The Christmas Special Christmas Special."

The King Family has recently produced a new public television special, their first in three decades, the first ever CD releases of their albums, and a planned return to the concert stage. There have been many changes and additions to the family over the past four decades (the head count at a recent family reunion exceeded 150!) but one thing has remained the same over the years—their love of being together as a family. And whether it's a warm and cozy Christmas caroling party, a niece's elegant wedding reception, or a good old-fashioned Fourth of July picnic, there is always an abundance of enticing and delicious home-cooked food around, from the wonderful recipes that have become part of this family's tradition.

INTRODUCTION

It all began with Pearl and King Driggs, who married in 1908 and had eight children: Karleton, Maxine, Luise, Alyce, Donna, Vonnie, Bill, and Marilyn. Each of those children married and had their own progeny, and King and Pearl's legacy continues through their children and their children's children today. The family is now at five generations and still expanding.

(Note: When King and Pearl's daughters started to sing professionally, they called themselves "The Driggs Sisters," but soon decided to adopt their father's first name for a more commercial-sounding "King Sisters.")

Pearl was a simple cook back when she raised her family in the 20's and 30's. She knew how to make good "Mormon" comfort food . . . gravy, pie crust, potatoes. She could season pretty well with just salt, pepper, and onions. With ten hungry mouths to feed there was never a morsel left, and dessert was carefully rationed out.

Pearl's children, more cultured and somewhat more financially stable, began to explore their culinary senses. Donna's flair was in the carb/sugar areas – great chocolate desserts, masses of mayonnaise, and piles of whipped cream. Vonnie's recipes were more exotic and always looked as fabulous as they tasted. To this day, her food presentations beat anything you'd see on one of the food networks. They conjure up visions of a beautiful table setting with the china, napkins, and centerpiece all perfectly color coordinated to fit the room's decor. Even if only serving a glass of orange juice, there is always a sprig of mint on the coaster.

Luise, along with her husband, Alvino, were fabulous gourmet chefs and passed their talent and love of food down to their children. Alyce was a great cook when she was hosting a party, but eventually moved more into the manufactured food products. Her son, Cam, claims that his particular favorite was "a great Swanson's entrée wrapped in frozen foil." Her specialties often included anything made by a man named Stouffer. Maxine cooked everything well, learning her mother's secrets for delicious home-made fare. Marilyn could create a great "spread," as the parties were often at her house. Her children enjoyed picnics and creative vacation foods. Karleton and Billy may not have learned to cook like their sisters, but they married great cooks, Hazel and Phyllis.

Holidays were always like major therapeutic medicine for the King Family. Holidays meant parties, and parties meant fabulous food. And many favorite family traditions were centered around the menus . . . like on Christmas mornings:

Karleton's family's traditional breakfast was homemade eggnog (better known as "fat-in-a-cup"); homemade Belgian Waffles with maple syrup, powdered sugar, whipped cream, and sliced strawberries; scrambled eggs, bacon and sausage; homemade cinnamon rolls, glazed or frosted; and orange juice.

Maxine – Orange juice and sweet rolls in the children's rooms while Mom and Dad prepared the "scene." After presents, scrambled eggs, bacon, toast, orange juice, and always a half of grapefruit neatly sectioned with a cherry on top.

Luise – Christmas bread, hot chocolate, gingerbread men, baked apples, and creamed chipped beef on toast.

Alyce – fruit cocktail (fruit was partially frozen so still a bit crunchy when sparkling cider was poured over it), Eggs

Benedict and ham on English muffins with hollandaise sauce, home fried potatoes.

Donna – orange juice, ½ grapefruit topped with thawed, frozen strawberries, creamed chipped beef on toast, Jones Little sausages, bacon, hot chocolate, Stouffer's Pecan Sweet Rolls, and of course, See's Chocolates.

Vonnie – gourmet Christmas "Snausages" in white wine, bright red cinnamon baked apples with whipped cream, scrambled eggs with cream cheese, bacon, sweet rolls and muffins with butter and jam, French hot chocolate.

Billy – orange juice and blueberry muffins to start. After gifts were opened then Abelskiver Pancakes (round like a ball) with applesauce inside served with butter, powdered sugar, more applesauce, and jam; bacon or sausage.

Marilyn – peeled and sliced oranges on a platter sprinkled with powdered sugar, Stouffer's Chipped Beef on English muffins, hot chocolate with mini marshmallows, and sweet rolls (made from the recipe on the Aunt Jemima's pancake box).

The rule of thumb for the King Family was that you could never work too hard on a meal or its presentation. Why wouldn't you want to bring your pewter dishes to the mountains and hang a pewter chandelier on a pine tree? Why wouldn't you include your crystal candelabras in your picnic basket at the beach? As Donna always said, "If your life is the same every day, you will have no memories. You have to go to a little trouble to make the day unique enough to be memorable." (See, Mom, we were listening!)

For the King Family, the presentation of the food is of equal importance to its taste. It's okay to use paper plates and napkins, but never with company. After all, what are all those silver chafing dishes, crystal goblets, and china platters in the cupboard for, if not to use - even for a grandmother's 80th birthday party or a daughter's bridal shower?

There are definite King Family rules of etiquette when it comes to cooking:

- Candles should not only be on the table, but lit.
- Lettuce should be torn, not cut (secretly, some probably cut lettuce, but never in front of another family member).
- It doesn't matter how rich the dessert already is, always use whipped cream because, according to Donna, "Whipped cream cuts the richness."
- You can never eat too much. (We're reminded of the time on "Summer Tour" when we stopped for lunch at a grocery store, and people came out with box loads of groceries…just for lunch!)
- You can never work too hard on making a meal a special occasion.
- The table should be properly set, and a centerpiece is a requirement (preferably fresh flowers from your own garden).
- There must be a variety of food colors on the plate.
- Everything needs nuts.
- Never stop with salt and pepper. Remember beau monde, tarragon, bouquet garni, saffron, curry, and paprika.
- It is, according to Vonnie, okay to use processed food, as long as you "doctor" it a little. If there is a great canned soup or vegetable or a packaged seasoning mix, use it. (See Vonnie's Minestrone Soup.) You can't make homemade Welsh rarebit better than Stouffer's.
- Never follow the directions on recipes for the seasonings. Always adjust and season to taste.
- Always ice the glasses when serving a cold beverage. Serve the salad on a chilled plate with an iced fork.
- Have parties. They're the things you'll remember at the end of your life.
- Margarine is a 4-letter word.

- And finally, Lawry's® Seasoned Salt **IS** salt!

Editor's Notes:

When the cookbook idea was instigated, there were many traditional family recipes that were in high demand. Hopefully all those demands have been satisfied. Some recipes will read like a conversation. You can hear Pearl and Vonnie and Donna discussing "Divinity" in that recipe. As recipes were submitted, it was amusing to see how many people claimed to have personally created the exact same recipe as another sister or cousin, who had submitted it as their original creation. How many people claimed they invented Mayonnaise Cake or Mandarin Orange Salad or Hot Chicken Salad? So to be fair, we have listed multiple contributors for certain recipes.

When the recipes started coming in, we feared that our family had rejected its true heritage. Suddenly the amount of "main dishes" far exceeded the category we thought would be the most jam-packed. But eventually our true roots began to spread forth. After all, Bob Mackie (our costume designer for our T.V. series) didn't create those diagonal lines on our dresses just for fun. Those lines were designed to cover up our family's true weakness . . . the love of eating sinfully rich foods! So, yes, our dessert category eventually caught up and far surpassed the others (there are 39 recipes listing chocolate as an ingredient!) By the way, Bob Mackie's job would become much easier in future years when he started designing costumes for Cher!

It's interesting that out of all of Tina's recipes, which are full of wonderfully rich ingredients, only one of her titles carries the word that traditionally describes her cooking – "Fagaga" (pronounced fah-gah-gah). But whether the recipes include butter and cream or all fresh, healthy vegetables, for us they conjure up visions of family get-togethers full of love and laughter.

Our family is as diverse now as any family could be . . . from the things we do to the philosophies by which we live . . . and that's okay. Because the thread of love that emanates from each of us and weaves us together as we sit around a beautiful table of yummy home-cooked food will bind us together forever.

"The King Family Show" 1965

"The King Family Show" 1969

CELEBRATE WITH THE KING FAMILY
Suggested Menus for Your Own Special Celebrations

    The King Family is a family on a mission: What is the next excuse we can think of to have a family party? Amazingly, we have yet to become sick of each other, and we live for the next time we can all be together. As our family is now stretched out across the nation from Maine to Los Angeles, from Dallas to Sacramento, from Salt Lake City to Phoenix, and all points in between, we continue to make great efforts to gather together.

    Until twenty years ago, we all lived within fifteen minutes of each other in the San Fernando Valley (near Los Angeles). So our party celebrations and menus were a continuing tradition. As we've moved apart, those traditional meals have a tight hold in our memories, and it's difficult to break a winning streak. We have included here some of our favorite celebration menus. You will find a recipe in our cookbook for almost all of the recipes mentioned below. Maybe you can borrow some of our memories to enhance traditions of your own . . . or create new traditions that incorporate your own family's culture and celebration style.

EASTER (or any SPRING CELEBRATION):
Ham and Turkey
Carrot Soufflé (p. 128)
Picnic Baked Beans (p. 127)
Broccoli Salad (p. 90)
Watermelon chunks (squeezed with fresh lemon juice, sprinkled with minced fresh mint leaves, tossed and chilled)
Lemon-Plum Tour Cake (p. 154)
Easter chocolates

MOTHER'S DAY BREAKFAST:
Tina's German Pancakes served with all the suggested condiments (p. 119)
Bacon and/or Sausage
Vonnie's Scrambled Eggs (p. 117)
Sparkling Apple Cider mixed with orange juice and a sprig of mint on top
Note: *Don't forget to serve your mother using your best china, prettiest napkin, and use lots of fresh flowers.*

MEMORIAL DAY PICNIC:
Tri-tip steak cooked on the BBQ with Driggsus Carnivorous Tri-Tip Steak Seasoning (p. 15)
Potatoes Oliver (p. 130) or fried potatoes with green onions cooked in a skillet over a BBQ
Mixed fresh fruit salad
Crusty French bread warmed on the BBQ
Aunt Lilly's Mayonnaise Cake (p. 141)
Richie King Clarke's Homemade Vanilla Ice Cream (p. 180)

FOURTH OF JULY:

BBQ Beef Sandwiches (p. 16)

Yummy Corn (p. 125) or corn on the cob

Coleslaw made your favorite way

Summer melons

Homemade Fruit Ice Cream (p. 178) topped with fresh strawberries and bananas with Fudge-Topped Brownies (p. 182) on the side

WEDDING/BABY SHOWER:

King Sisters '50s Luncheon Sandwich Loaf (p. 114)

Strawberry Spinach Salad (p. 101)

Baked Fruit (p. 132)

Chocolate Torte (p. 161)

Lime Cucumber Punch (p. 205)

AUTUMN CELEBRATION:

Tina's Norwegian Cauliflower Soup (p. 82)

Broccoli Cheese Soup (p. 78)

Winter Salad with Pears (p. 100)

Ham and Cheese Round (p. 216)

Hot Holiday Cider (p. 202)

Pumpkin Surprise (p. 139)

Marilyn King, Kent Larsen & the boy cousins on the "September with the King Family" TV special 1968

THANKSGIVING:

Turkey, gravy, and cranberries/cranberry sauce
Dressing fixed your favorite way
Candied Sweet Potatoes and Apples (p. 131)
Fresh Green Beans (p. 126)
Carolyn's Dinner Rolls (p. 228)
Pumpkin pie, Apple pie, Chocolate Silk Pie (p. 166) and Pumpkin Cake (p. 152)
Note: *King Family desserts always include some kind of chocolate and all desserts are topped with fresh, whipped cream.*

CHRISTMAS DAY (or any WINTER CELEBRATION):

Breakfast:
Vonnie's Gourmet Christmas Snausages (p. 116)
Vonnie's Scrambled Eggs (p. 117)
Spiced Apples served cold with whipped cream (p. 115)
Your favorite sweet roll or coffee cake
Gourmet Hot Chocolate (p. 203)

Dinner:
Tina's Shepherd's Pie (p. 18)
King Family Mandarin Orange Salad (p. 104)
Carolyn's Dinner Rolls (p. 228)
Trifle Christmas Pudding (p. 140)

Performing on the "Christmas with the King Family" TV special 1967

Main Dishes

The King Family, circa 1967

TINA'S BEEF STROGANOFF
(Tina Cole)
Simple to make and simply the best!

Serves 4-6

1 ½ lbs. filet (or other tender) steak, cut into 2"x12" thin strips
1 cup brown gravy packet (Knorr, Shilling, etc) and follow directions on packet

¼ cup butter
2 Tbsp. chopped yellow onion
3 large mushrooms, thinly sliced
1 tsp. salt
½ tsp. Pepper
1 pkg. thin egg noodles or rice

1 cup Half & Half
1 cup sour cream
½ cup sherry wine
½ cup chives, chopped
3 Tbsp. flour

Combine and blend brown gravy, cream, sour cream, and sherry until smooth. Set aside. Heat butter in skillet and sauté onions for 2 minutes. Add meat, mushrooms, salt and pepper and sauté on high heat for 3 - 4 minutes, turning meat over just until no longer pink. Remove from heat. Sprinkle with flour. Stir until paste. Return to high heat and cook 1 minute. Pour gravy/cream mixture and ¼ cup of chives over meat and lower heat to medium. Stir and bring just to a boil. Serve over noodles or rice. Top with dollop of sour cream and sprinkling of chives.

Tina with son Volney on "Christmas with the King Family" 1967

DRIGGSUS CARNIVOROUS TRI-TIP STEAK, BEEF ROAST, OR PORK ROAST SEASONING

(Ric de Azevedo)

Driggs is our grandfather's name, and let's face it – we all love an occasional good piece of red meat. Ric is recognized by our family as the king of the BBQ because of his expertise in seasoning and knowing when the meat is done!

Sprinkle or rub liberally:
Lawry's Seasoned Salt
Garlic Powder (not Garlic Salt) - lots of it
Coarse Ground Black Pepper
That's it!! ! !

For a variation, drizzle a little Lea & Perrin's Original Worcestershire Sauce on meat before adding dry seasonings. Be careful, a little Lea & Perrins goes a long way.

King Cousin Ric de Azevedo at the BBQ in the late '70s

BARBEQUE BEEF FOR SANDWICHES
(Jamie Miller)
Great for a casual buffet in the summertime

Serves 12

4 lb. cross-rib roast
    or any other inexpensive boneless beef roast
Hamburger buns or rolls (cold or warmed)

1 onion, quartered	¼ cup Worcestershire sauce
1 Tbsp. Lawry's	2 Tbsp. A-1 Sauce
½ tsp. garlic powder	1 can beef bouillon
½ tsp. pepper	Your favorite bottled BBQ Sauce
¼ cup wine vinegar	

Place roast and first 8 ingredients in prepared cellophane roasting bag in a 9x13 roasting pan (or put directly in pan, cover tightly with foil, poke holes in foil) and bake. (Cooking options: 250°– 8 hrs; 300°– 6 hrs) Remove from oven. Pour off liquid into a separate container. Remove fat and shred meat. Add BBQ Sauce to taste and portion of remaining juice as needed for desired moistness, serving leftover juice as "au jus" with sandwiches. Serve shredded meat on rolls with BBQ Sauce and desired condiments.

Sisters, Candy Brand, Jamie Miller and Xan Albright - daughters of Donna & Jim Conkling - at a mid '60s family gathering

BARBEQUE BEEF OR PORK ALTERNATE
(Laurette Walton)

This is completely different than our King Family traditional way of preparing BBQ beef – but sometimes you've got to break away!

Serves 10-12

5-6 lb. Boston Pork Butt or Chuck Roast
2 medium onions
6 cloves
2 Bay Leaves

Cover meat with other ingredients and cover with water, cooking in a large kettle until tender, 2 ½-3 ½ hours. Shred meat. (You can also cook meat in a bag in oven but this way is better for this recipe)

Sauce:

1 onion, chopped	⅔ cup dark brown sugar
2 Tbsp. butter	¼ cup Worcestershire sauce
2 ½ cups ketchup	1 Tbsp. salt
1 cup vinegar	2 Tbsp. pepper (or less, to taste)
1 cup water	2 Tbsp. chili powder (or less, to taste)

Sauté onion in butter in saucepan. Add remaining ingredients. Cover and cook low 30 minutes. Put ½ of the sauce in the shredded meat and use the remaining sauce on the buns if using for sandwiches. It is fairly spicy but sweet and yummy too!

TINA'S SHEPHERD'S PIE
(Tina Cole)

This is served at all her Christmas parties and has become her traditional Christmas Eve dinner. It's much simpler than it looks!

In 1972, Tina and Cathy Cole thought it would be great fun to have an intimate dinner party with a few of their professional singer friends to sing in rich harmony the season's Christmas Carols, old and new. The intimate party exploded to 85 people, 50 of whom were family members. Tina remembered a simple peasant dish that her son's English nanny had prepared with hamburger, called Shepherd's Pie, and that clinched it. It would be an old fashioned English Caroling Party.

Invitations were sent out to attend the 1st Annual Cratchett Christmas Choir's Feast and Fest. Everyone was to "Dress like the Dickens!" And they did – from St. Nicholas to Lords and Ladies, from street urchins to the Ghosts of Christmas Past! For the dinner, Tina created her own "gourmet" version of Shepherd's Pie, making it look like "Old King Cole's Pie," and large enough to serve 30 people. She made four of these huge, incredibly delicious pies and the guests thought they had died and gone to heaven – there wasn't one pea left in any of the pans.

After dinner, everyone gathered together with just the glow from the fire, the candles, lighted garlands and Christmas tree, and sang their hearts out for hours! For nine years this annual party became for many the…"now it feels like Christmas" moment. One year Tina even surprised everyone by getting married to her TV mother-in-law, Beverly Garland's son, right in the middle of the caroling! When Tina moved to Sacramento she continued the annual event for another twelve years. In her absence in Los Angeles, cousin Cam Clarke began his own annual caroling party, and it continues to this day.

Serves 30

Cookware:
16" cake pan with 3" sides (½ recipe fits 11x13 or 12" round)
1 large roasting bag
1 large roasting pan

1 large pot
1 small ceramic blackbird (used in fruit pies to release steam)

Part 1:
6 lb. boneless bottom round or chuck
1 large yellow onion, quartered
1 cup burgundy wine
2 cloves garlic, minced
¾ cup Worcestershire sauce
1 Tbsp. coarse ground pepper
1 Lipton onion soup mix pouch
1 can bouillon (concentrate)
1 Tbsp. Lawry's
2 bay leaves
⅓ cup A-1 Sauce

Part 2:
2 bags each, frozen "Parisienne" carrots (small round carrots – preferred) or baby carrots (par-cooked 10 minutes) and frozen "petite" peas

Part 3:
3 (15-oz.) boxes "Hungry Jack" (preferred) potato flakes:

(½ the amount of milk that's called for on package instructions. Water according to package instructions.)

3 Tbsp. Lawry's   1 tsp. white pepper
5 cubes butter   1 pint sour cream
3 Tbsp. onion powder

Part 4:
6 cups grated sharp cheddar cheese

To prepare:

Part 1: The night before, put "prepared" browning bag in baking dish. Add meat and ½ cup of wine, ½ the Worcestershire sauce, and ½ the can of bouillon. Add the rest of ingredients in part 1. Close bag with plastic tie. Cut 6 slits in top of bag. Cook at 225° for 6-8 hours. Go to bed. In the morning pour juice into large pot. Remove fat as you cut meat into bite size pieces. Set aside.

Part 2: Add rest of wine, Worcestershire sauce and bouillon to meat juice and bring to low boil. Add meat and cook 10 minutes. Add par-cooked carrots and cook 10 minutes more. Remove from heat and stir in peas. With a slotted spoon or strainer, scoop meat and veggies into bottom of cake pan, making sure the mixture is moist with juice but not swimming in it. Mixture should fill ⅔ of pan.

Part 3: In a large pot, boil water for potatoes. Add butter, milk and seasonings. Remove from heat and stir in sour cream. Whip in flakes until blended. Potatoes will be VERY stiff. Spread portion of potatoes over meat/veggies until they are level with top of pan. With damp hands, roll remaining potatoes into snake shape. Place around top outer edge of pan (edging) and make 4 spokes to center. Flute edges to look like a crust (don't hang over edge). Make a "well" in the center of spokes to place blackbird after pie is cooked.

Part 4: Sprinkle cheese in each space between spokes. Sprinkle whole pie with paprika. Spread foil in bottom of oven for drips. Bake at 350° approx. 1 hour (potatoes start to golden). Before serving, place ceramic blackbird (used in fruit pies to release steam) for decoration in center of pie.

TINA'S PILGRIM'S PIE
(Tina Cole)
Just like Shepherd's Pie, but for "non-beef eaters"

Serves 30

Cookware:

16" cake pan with 3" sides (½ recipe fits 11x13 or 12" round)

1 large roasting bag

1 large roasting pan

1 large pot

Part 1:

1 (12-oz.) box Stove Top Stuffing

2 green apples peeled & cubed

6 slices bacon

6 mushrooms sliced

1 med. onion, chopped

2 cubes butter

3 ⅓ cups chicken broth or water

1 pkg. dried fruit bits or dried apricots, chopped

2 pieces celery, chopped

Salt, pepper, Lawry's, poultry seasoning to taste

(or if using leftovers - 1 ½ quarts homemade stuffing)

Part 2:

5 lbs. cooked turkey, bite size chunks

1 qt. turkey gravy

½ cup sherry wine or cooking sherry

⅓ cup Worcestershire sauce

¼ cup A-1 Sauce

2 bags each, frozen "Parisienne" carrots (small round carrots – preferred) or baby carrots (par-cooked 10 minutes) and frozen "petite" peas

Part 3:
3 (15-oz.) boxes "Hungry Jack" (preferred) potato flakes:
(½ the amount of milk that's called for on package instructions. Water according to package instructions.)

3 Tbsp. Lawry's
5 cubes butter
3 Tbsp. onion powder
1 pint sour cream
1 tsp. white pepper

Part 4:
3 cans whole berry cranberry sauce, stirred

To prepare:

Part 1: Fry bacon in large pan until crisp; remove to paper towel and crumble. Add 1 cube butter to bacon fat and sauté onions, celery, apples, and mushrooms. Bring water or broth to a boil and add remaining cube of butter and all seasonings (including the stuffing packet) stirring to blend. Pour stuffing in a large bowl and pour in liquid, vegetables, fruit bits and bacon. Toss until stuffing is just moist and pat into bottom of 16" cake pan.

Part 2: In large pot bring turkey gravy, sherry, Worcestershire, and A-1 to a low boil. Add turkey and cook 10 min. Add par-cooked carrots, cook 10 minutes more. Remove from heat and stir in peas. Using a slotted spoon or strainer, place meat/veggie over stuffing layer making sure the meat is moist with the gravy but not swimming in it. Mixture should fill ⅔ of pan.

Part 3: Boil water in a large pot. Add butter, milk, seasonings. Remove from heat and stir in sour cream. Whip in flakes until blended. Potatoes should be VERY stiff. Spread portion of potatoes over turkey/veggie layer until they are level with top of pan. With moist hands, roll remaining potatoes into snake shape and place around outer edge of pan and make 4 spokes to the center. Flute potato edge like a crust, but do not hang over the sides.

Part 4: Stir cranberry sauces together and spoon into the 4 wedges of the spokes. Spread foil in bottom of oven for drips. Bake at 350° for 1 hour until potatoes start to golden. Before serving, place ceramic blackbird (used in fruit pies to release steam) for decoration in center of pie.

SPICY GARLIC PRIME RIB EYE FEAST
(Dale Foshée)

Serve 8 or more

5-7 lbs. Prime Rib Eye - bone out
16 oz. Dijon mustard (Grey Poupon)
16 oz. soy sauce
¼ cup Montreal Steak Seasoning
4 tsp. balsamic vinegar
4 green onions, chopped
4 Tbsp. Hot Chili Garlic Sauce (Tuong Ot Toi - Vietnamese)

In a 9x13 Pyrex, rub quite a bit of the soy sauce and Montreal Steak Seasoning (cover the meat with the Montreal Seasoning) all over the rib eye and wrap it up in saran overnight. Next day – Mix the mustard, any remaining soy sauce, the Hot Chili Sauce (add more if you dare!), and the vinegar. Mix well and pour over marinated meat. Cover the meat with foil and bake for 2 hours at 350°. Put the rib eye on the grill and finish the cooking by grilling it to medium-medium rare. Remove, add the green onions and pour the sauce on top. Cut into 6-8 steaks, 1½ inches thick. Awesome!

SWEET MEATLOAF
(Kelly Miller)

Serves 6

½ cup brown sugar
½ cup ketchup
1½ lbs lean ground beef
1 small onion, chopped
¼ tsp. ground ginger
2 eggs
¾ cup milk
1½ tsp. salt
¼ tsp. ground black pepper
¾ cup finely crushed Saltine cracker crumbs

Lightly grease 5x9 loaf pan. Press brown sugar into the bottom of the pan and spread ketchup over the sugar. In a bowl, mix all remaining ingredients and place on top of ketchup in the shape of a loaf. Bake at 350° for 1 hour or until juices are clear.

FLANK STEAK MARINADE
(Laurette Walton)

Serves 4

1½ lbs. flank steak

Marinade:
¼ c. vegetable oil
2 Tbsp. soy sauce
1 Tbsp. cider vinegar
1 Tbsp. honey
1 chopped scallion
1 garlic clove, minced
⅛ tsp. ginger
1 tsp. Lawry's
Pepper

Meat: Prick holes in steak with a fork and marinade in a 9x13 for several hours. To cook steak, grill for about 7 min per side or until desired doneness. Slice against the grain, into thin strips.

KOREAN STEAK SKEWERS

(Jamie Miller)

Serves 4

1 scored flank steak
3 Tbsp. sesame seeds
¼ cup salad oil
½ cup soy sauce
2 cloves crushed garlic
½ tsp. pepper
½ tsp. ginger
¼ cup brown sugar
2 green onions, sliced

Mix all ingredients except steak. Pour over meat in glass dish. Marinate overnight. Can be cut into strips and put on skewers. Broil about 5 minutes (or barbeque). Can be served as appetizers or meat entree.

SWEDISH MEATBALLS

(Cheryl Driggs)

Serves 10

2 ½ lbs. ground beef
2 cans beef bouillon
½ cup butter
4 eggs
1 cup bread crumbs
1 cup finely chopped onion
2 cans cream of mushroom soup
2 cups sour cream
2 cups milk
3 tsp. salt
¼ tsp. each of nutmeg, allspice, cardamom

Cook onions in 2 Tbsp. of the butter until soft. Beat eggs slightly and mix with milk, onions and bread crumbs. Add salt, spices, and beef and knead until mixed. Mixture will be soft. Chill at least 1 hour. Shape into 1" balls. In skillet melt remaining butter and brown slowly, turning so they hold shape. As they brown, arrange in a casserole or Dutch oven. Remove drippings from pan except for ¼ cup. Stir in soup and bouillon. Stir constantly on low setting. Gently fold in sour cream. Pour sauce over meatballs. Heat at 350° for 30-40 minutes. Serve over noodles.

BEEFY BEAN BAKE

(Chick Rey)

These are a hit at any family picnic!

Serves 12

½ lb. ground beef
10 slices bacon, chopped
½ cup chopped onion
¼ cup ketchup
¼ cup BBQ sauce
2 Tbsp. molasses
2 Tbsp. prepared mustard
1 (16 oz) can kidney beans, drained
1 (16 oz) can pork & beans, undrained
1 (16 oz) can butter beans, drained

⅓ cup white sugar
⅓ cup brown sugar
½ tsp. chili powder
½ tsp. salt
½ tsp. black pepper

Brown meats, drain. Add onion and cook until tender. Add sugars and seasonings; then add beans. Pour into 9x13 or large round casserole. Bake at 350° for 1 hour.

King Sister Yvonne aka Vonnie with her famous pewter table settings on the beach at a family picnic

ALVINO'S FAMOUS GREEK LEG OF LAMB ROAST
(Alvino Rey)

Alvino was the true gourmet of the family. When we were doing our "one-nighter" bus tours, Alvino would re-route the bus a hundred miles out of the way, just so we could stop for dinner at some "great Greek restaurant" or the "best Crayfish restaurant in Louisiana."

This recipe of Alvino and Luise's came from Alvino's guitar teacher, Sophocles Pappas, who was also the teacher for the world's greatest classical guitarist, Andres Segovia. The famous leg of lamb became a "Homecoming" dinner that Alvino and Luise often prepared when any of their kids had been away from home and returned. It was always a celebration!

Alvino created an entire Greek dinner which was featured in the Salt Lake Tribune in the 1980's. The recipes are included throughout this cookbook. They are: Alvino's Leg of Lamb, Spinach Feta Pie, Greek Lemon Rice Soup, and Feta Salad. This dinner was voted the "Best Recipe of the Year" by the Tribune readers.

Rosemary
Salt and pepper
Walnut sauce (Cross and Blackwell's recommended)
Mint sauce and Red wine
Small cooked new red potatoes
Small cooked fresh carrots
Small cooked white onions
Lawry's

Score lamb roast with knife in six places; insert cloves of garlic in cuts. Season lamb with crushed bay leaf, oregano and salt and pepper as desired. Bake at 350° for 1-2 hours. Add walnut sauce, mint sauce and wine as desired. (Vonnie claims apple/mint jelly is the correct choice for lamb!) Place cooked vegetables around roast. Baste vegetables with juices from lamb roast and bake for an additional hour, covered, at 350°. Season vegetables with Lawry's and pepper. To serve, place lamb roast in center of platter. Position cooked, basted vegetables around roast. Serve with pride.

BARBECUED PORK RIBS
(Carla Rey)

Serves 2
1 rack of baby back ribs or 1 rack or pork ribs, skinned
2 Tbsp. olive oil
2 garlic cloves, crushed
1 tsp. salt
1 tsp. black pepper, crushed
2 Tbsp. honey
1 Tbsp. fresh parsley, chopped

Mix together ingredients and brush on the ribs. Cook in 250° oven for one hour. Cool and refrigerate.

To barbecue: Place ribs on the barbecue and brush with sauce. Cook, turn, and baste for 15 min. or until done.

Barbecue Sauce--Mix all together:
½ cup bottled barbecue sauce – your choice
½ cup fresh pineapple, chopped
 2 Tbsp. soy sauce
 Pinch of chili powder

PULLED SWEET PORK
(Kelly Miller)

Serves 6

2 lbs. boneless pork rib meat or roast
1¼ cups brown sugar
3 cans Coke or Dr. Pepper (NOT diet)
Dash of garlic salt
¼ cup water
7 oz. can diced green chilies
¾ can enchilada sauce, mild or medium
1 cup brown sugar (used later)

Marinate the pork for a few hours or overnight in a heavy duty Ziploc bag with 1½ cans Coke and brown sugar. Drain marinade and put pork, ½ can of Coke, water, and garlic salt in Crockpot on high for 3-4 hours, until it shreds easily but is not dry (or on low for 8 hours). Remove pork; drain and discard any excess liquid. Shred the pork. In a food processor or blender, blend ½ can Coke, chilies, enchilada sauce and 1 cup brown sugar. If it looks too thick, add more Coke, a little at a time. Return the pork and the sauce to Crockpot and cook on low for 2 hours. Serve the meat with salad and vegetables or use for tacos, burritos, or salad.

King fathers LaVarn Thomas, Bob Clarke and Alvino Rey, man the BBQ at Casa Las Posas - Alvino & Luise's Camarillo, CA home

PORK CHOPS WITH APPLES AND STUFFING
(Donna Thomas)

Serves 6

6 boneless pork loin chops, 1 inch thick
1 pkg. (6 oz.) stuffing mix
2 Tbsp. minced onion
1 Tbsp. vegetable oil
Ingredients on package to make stuffing
1 can (21 oz.) apple pie filling with cinnamon

In a skillet, brown pork chops and onion in oil over medium-high heat. Meanwhile, prepare stuffing according to package directions. Spread pie filling into a greased 9x13 baking dish. Place the pork chops on top; spoon stuffing over chops. Cover and bake at 350° for 35 minutes. Uncover; bake 10 minutes longer or until a meat thermometer reads 160°.

BERRIED PORK TENDERLOIN
(Candy Brand)

Serves 6

2-3 lbs. pork tenderloin
1 pkg. Lipton's dry onion soup
1 can whole cranberry sauce
18 oz. bottle of Catalina dressing
1 pkg (6 oz) Stove Top Stuffing mix

Place the tenderloin in a 9X13 Pyrex. Mix the soup, cranberries, and dressing together and pour over the pork. Bake at 400° for 1¼ hours. Serve over Stove Top Stuffing, drizzled with drippings and cranberries.

ROCKY MOUNTAIN RIBS
(Jani Driggs)

Serves 6-8
3 pounds boneless ribs (pork or beef)
Sauce:

2 Tbsp. cornstarch　　　　1 cup catsup
1⅛ cup brown sugar　　　½ cup water
1 tsp. salt　　　　　　　　¼ cup vinegar
½ tsp. celery salt　　　　　¼ cup soy sauce
½ Tbsp. chili powder　　　2 Tbsp. liquid smoke

Bring sauce to a boil and add raw ribs. Simmer for 2 hours and serve with rice.

BARBECUED CHICKEN PIZZA
(Xan Albright)
A quick family dinner favorite!

Serves 6
2-3 chicken breasts
1 frozen bread dough loaf (like Bridgford's), thawed
BBQ sauce of choice
½ - 1 lb. grated Jack cheese
1 bunch cilantro, chopped (optional…but it's the best part!)

Cook chicken breasts (preferably grilled), brushing BBQ sauce on them and then cut in small pieces. Roll thawed dough into circular or rectangular pizza shape and put on round pizza pan or cookie sheet. Brush a good amount of BBQ sauce onto the dough. On top sprinkle chicken, cilantro, and cheese. Bake at 425° for 15-20 minutes until bubbly.

CATHY'S PASTA BROCCOLI WITH TURKEY MEAT SAUCE
(Cathy Green)
Good for a crowd. Delicious!

Serves 4-6

1-1½ lbs. ground turkey (thigh is best, or use part white meat)

Sauce:
2 Tbsp. olive oil	½ Tbsp. butter
½ cup chopped onion	½ Tbsp. sugar
¼ cup red wine	¼ cup heavy cream

3-4 cloves fresh garlic, peeled and lightly crushed
1 jar Classico Ripe Olive and Mushroom Sauce

Heat olive oil and butter in large skillet. Sauté onion and garlic until translucent. Add turkey and cook until done, but not overdone, stirring to break up into little crumbles. Drain oil. Add sauce, wine, sugar and blend. Simmer for 15 minutes. Add cream, blend, and simmer low for 30-45 minutes more.

Pasta and Broccoli:
1 box fusilli, rotini, or spaghetti	1¼ cup butter
1 large bunch broccoli florets	¼ cup olive oil
2-3 cloves lightly crushed garlic	Parmesan cheese, shredded
⅓ cup freshly squeezed lemon juice	

Cook pasta in salted water as directed. Keep al dente. Steam lightly salted broccoli. Should look very green, don't overcook. Put butter, olive oil, and garlic in a Pyrex cup and microwave until butter melts, approx. 1 minute on high. Remove garlic cloves. When pasta and broccoli are done, drain pasta. Put in large bowl or back in pot. Add broccoli and toss with melted butter mixture and lemon juice. Sprinkle with Parmesan cheese. Serve with turkey meat sauce on the side, Italian salad, and hot sourdough bread.

HOT CHICKEN "SALAD" (AKA "Chicken Surprise")
(Donna King Conkling, Donna Thomas)

Serves 8

3 stewed chicken breasts, cut up
1 can water chestnuts, sliced
1 can cream of chicken soup
1 cup celery, chopped
2 cups potato chips, crushed
⅓ cup sliced almonds
1 Tbsp. lemon juice
1 cup mayonnaise
½ carrot, diced

Mix everything except potato chips and put in a greased 2-quart casserole. Top with crushed potato chips. Bake at 350° for 30 minutes.

TARRAGON CHICKEN
(Donna King Conkling)

A clay pot, Dutch oven, or baking dish with a tight lid is needed for this recipe.

Serves 4-6

Roasting chicken (or 3 whole chicken breasts)
3 shallots or green onions, chopped
½ cup chicken broth or bouillon+water

1 Tbsp. parsley
Salt and pepper
2 Tbsp. flour
½ pint heavy cream
1 bay leaf
3 Tbsp. butter
2 Tbsp. lemon juice
½ cup white wine
½ tsp. thyme

Sauté onions in butter. Add wine, broth, and seasonings. Simmer 3 minutes. Season chicken with salt and pepper. Place chicken in clay pot, cover with the liquid. Cover and cook 400° for 1 hour. Pour lemon juice over chicken, cover and cook ½ -1 hour more. Remove chicken – wrap in foil to keep hot. Put juices in skillet with heavy cream. Make a roux with flour and water and whisk into juices and cream. Simmer until thickened. Serve over chicken. So delicious!

CHICKEN À LA KING

(Phyllis Heim, Yvonne King Burch, Tina Cole)

This is our collective favorite Christmas night main dish. For years, each family had their own Christmas morning and couldn't wait to get together with the "big" family on Christmas night to show off special gifts, to eat, play games, and – you guessed it – sing!

Serves 15

3 cups cooked Chicken, cubed
Frozen Pepperidge Farm Patty Shells
1 bag frozen petite peas (optional)
1½ cups chicken broth
3 cups Half & Half or whole milk
1 Tbsp. salt
1 cup sliced mushrooms
⅓ cup each sliced pimientos
1 cup + 2 Tbsp. butter
1½ tsp. white pepper
1 cup + 2 Tbsp. flour
3 Tbsp butter
½ cup sherry
Lawry's Season Salt to taste
½ cup each: chopped onion & green peppers

In a small pan, sauté butter with onions, peppers, and mushrooms and set aside. In a large pot over medium heat, melt butter and stir in flour to make a roux. Slowly add broth and half & half, stirring constantly until thickened and smooth. Stir in remaining ingredients, except peas and Lawry's, and cook 10 minutes, stirring often to keep from scorching. Remove from burner and stir in peas, then Lawry's to taste. Return to heat only long enough to bring up temperature if needed. Serve over Pepperidge Farm Patty Shells or biscuits, baked according to instructions.

APPLE CURRY CHICKEN
(The Fabulous Miss Vonnie)

When Vonnie asked her husband Bill what he'd like for his birthday dinner, he simply answered, "Curry would be kind of nice."

With that, Vonnie's creative wheels began to spin. Searching from store to store, she collected 50 yards of peach silk at a closeout sale, 20 wooden apple crates to use as seats, which she painted Mandarin Red, and paisley bedspreads from India, which she made into matching pillows in the party colors of peach, lilac, and apple green. Her sons-in-law were called to empty her living room of its furniture. The peach silk was draped to create a huge tent. She rented a long table and laid plaid silk runners down the center. She set the table with gold lacquered plates, brass candlesticks of every size, and crystal bowls filled with roses in all her party colors. After the exotic food Vonnie prepared had been served, she brought in hot, perfumed finger towels. Bill commented that the night was wonderful and beautiful, but all he had said was… "Curry would be nice."

Serves 6-8

6 cups cubed chicken or turkey AND the broth
   (or use canned broth)

3 cups milk	6 Tbsp. butter
2 thin slices garlic	2 bay leaves
12 thin slices onion	1 cup onion chopped
8 sprigs fresh parsley	4 Tbsp. flour
4 tsp. curry powder	1 tsp. salt

2 cups chopped Pippin apples
Dash of nutmeg & cayenne pepper

Step 1: Scald the milk with garlic, bay leaves onion and parsley. After scalding, strain all the spices/onions, etc from the milk (they were just for flavor) and set aside.

Step Two: Sauté onions and apples in butter until onions are transparent. Remove from heat.

Step Three: Mix together dry ingredients and sprinkle over apples and onions. Stir to blend, making a paste. Return to heat and while stirring constantly, slowly pour in strained, scalded milk from Step 1, and enough broth to make into a gravy consistency. Bring to a slow boil stirring constantly.

Step Four: Add chicken and let simmer until heated. Serve over rice with these condiments:

Finely sliced green onions
Raisins
Mandarin oranges
Chopped hard-boiled eggs
Chutney
Cut pineapple
Chopped peanuts
Crisp bacon (crumbled)
Shaved coconut
Fresh lime wedges
Sliced bananas sprinkled with cinnamon

If you really want to be like Aunt Vonnie, you'll build a whole party around this recipe. You'll buy 25 yards of silk and make a tent inside your living room. Color coordinate the menu items and table décor to match the colors of the silk tent. (Make sure the colors are aubergine, celadon or ecru, not just some regular colors like purple, green or beige).

CAJUN CHICKEN

(Amy Nottingham)
Good with boiled potatoes

Serves 4

4 thawed chicken breasts
¼ tsp. cayenne pepper
¼ tsp. black pepper
¼ tsp. paprika
½ tsp. basil
½ tsp. garlic powder
¼ tsp. dry mustard
1 tsp. salt

Flour
2 Tbsp. butter
2 green onions, chopped
1 ½ cups chicken broth
1 Tbsp. cornstarch
3 Tbsp. cold water
2 Tbsp. sour cream

Mix spices. Dust both sides of chicken with spices, then flour. In large frying pan, cook chicken 3 minutes in butter, turn over and cook 3 more minutes. Add green onions, cook 1 minute. Add chicken broth and cook 6 minutes over med-low heat. Remove chicken and cover to keep warm. Heat broth for 3 minutes on high. Dissolve cornstarch in cold water and add to sauce. Cook 1 more minute. Let stand 2 min. Stir in sour cream.

King parents Kent Larsen, Alvino Rey, Yvonne King Burch, Bill Burch, Alyce King Clarke, Bob Clarke and Luise King Rey

CHICKEN MANDARIN
(Jamie Miller)

Serves 8

4-6 chicken breasts
2 cans cream of mushroom or cream of chicken soup
1 pkg. Lipton's onion soup mix
½ pint sour cream
¼ cup butter or margarine
1 tsp. Lawry's Seasoning Salt
¼ tbsp. pepper
1-2 small cans mandarin oranges
½ cup cooking sherry

Sauté thawed breasts in butter, seasoning salt and pepper 15 minutes. (You can also use chicken "tenders" or pieces instead of whole breasts.) Put in 9x13 casserole. Sprinkle with 1 packet of onion soup mix. Mix together soup mix, sherry, sour cream. Pour over the chicken. Bake 350° for ½ hour. Add oranges on top last 5-10 minutes. Serve over rice.

King Cousins Carolyn Cameron, Ray Driggs, Xan Albright, Tina Cole, Cathy Green & Jamie Miller backstage at a King Family concert with King Sister Yvonne peeking through

CHICKEN WITH PEPPERS AND SHERRY
(Laurette Walton)

Serves 4-6
4-6 boneless chicken breasts
1 each red, yellow, and green peppers
2 shallots
½ cup cooking sherry
2 Tbsp. butter
½ pint heavy cream
Lawry's seasoning salt, pepper

Heat butter in large skillet. Brown boneless, skinless chicken breasts for about 2 minutes a side, turning occasionally. Season with salt, pepper, Lawry's. Cut 4 peppers into strips (I use one of each color, red, yellow, green, or any combination is fine.) Scatter peppers and chopped shallots around the chicken. Cover and cook 5 minutes. Add sherry and cover and cook 10 minutes more on medium. Turn chicken and stir peppers occasionally so it cooks evenly. Transfer chicken to warm platter and cover with foil. Add up to a small container of heavy cream (up to 1 cup) to skillet. Continue cooking uncovered for about 5 minutes until cream is slightly reduced. Add chicken back into skillet to warm again and serve over rice.

Note: green peppers take the longest to cook, then red, then yellow so put green in first for a minute, then add red, then yellow.

CONKLING CHICKEN CRESCENT ROLL-UPS

(Xan Albright, Tina Cole)
*This is a perfect dinner to share with others
– even the children will love it!*

Serves 8

3-4 chicken breasts cooked and cubed
2 pkgs. Pillsbury Crescent Refrigerator Rolls
8 oz. cream cheese
½ cup milk
2 tsp. dried onion
5 Tbsp. butter
¾ cup chopped celery
½ tsp. Lawry's, pepper to taste
1 tsp. Bouquet Garni (optional)

Coating:
½ cup melted butter
½ cup seasoned bread crumbs blended
½ cup finely chopped pecans

Sauce:
Mix together in saucepan and cook until hot:
1 can cream of chicken soup
⅓ cup sherry wine or water
¼ cup sour cream
Fresh lemon juice to taste

Melt butter and reserve 2 Tbsp. for the topping. Mix together cream cheese, milk, celery, 3 Tbsp. of the butter, and seasonings. Add chicken and mix together. Separate crescent roll into 8 large rectangles (two triangles make 1 rectangle). Rectangles make adult portion; for children, just use the triangle. Press perforations together, sealing the seams. Scoop 1 to 2

Tbsp. chicken mix into center of roll, bring sides up together and twist at the top causing a little "knot" at the top. Dip the top of the filled roll into reserved melted butter (or brush it on) and then dip this top into bread crumbs blended with the pecans. Bake at 350° for 15 - 20 minutes until golden. Pour sauce over the top.

CHICKEN DIVAN
(Diana Driggs)

Serves 4-6

2 whole chicken breasts
1 cup bread crumbs
½ tsp. lemon juice
2 Tbsp. butter, melted
1 cup cheddar cheese, grated
1 can cream of chicken soup
1 bunch broccoli
½ cup mayonnaise
½ tsp. curry powder

Steam broccoli for 10 minutes. Boil chicken; cool and debone.

Place broccoli in bottom of a greased 8 inch pan, place chicken pieces over broccoli. Mix soup, mayonnaise, curry powder and lemon juice well and place this sauce over the chicken. Sprinkle grated cheese over the sauce. Mix melted butter with bread crumbs and place this over the cheese.
Bake for 30 minutes at 350°

WILSON SISTERS' ITALIAN CHICKEN
(Kristen, Brooke, and Noelle Wilson)

Serves 6

4-5 boneless, skinless chicken breasts (can be frozen)
1 (8 oz) package cream cheese
1 (10 oz) can cream of chicken
1 (10 oz) can cream of mushroom
1 package dried Italian dressing (like a Four Season's pkg.)

In large crockpot, combine chicken, cream cheese, soup, and dressing. Cook on high for 4 hours or low for 8 hours. Serve over rice. YUMMY!! Great "comfort food."

CRANBERRY CHICKEN
(Xan Albright)
This is beautiful at Christmas time.

Serves 6-8

6 frozen chicken breasts
¾ c. French or Catalina dressing
1 can whole cranberries w/ sauce
2 Tbsp. dried onion
2 Tbsp. Worcestershire

Mix ingredients and pour over frozen chicken in a 9x13 pan. Bake at 350° for 45 minutes covered. Then uncover and bake another 30 - 45 minutes. Serve over rice.

EXOTIC CHICKEN
(Tina Cole)

Tina got this recipe from her MY THREE SONS TV-mother-in-law-turned-real-life-mother-in-law, Beverly Garland

Serves 4-6

4-6 boneless, skinless chicken breasts
2 Tbsp. each- butter, olive oil
Lawry's, Pepper – to taste
14 oz. bottle of Russian dressing
1 jar apricot-pineapple preserves
1 packet Lipton Onion Soup mix

Sauté chicken in butter and oil until lightly browned. Season to taste. Place in 9X13 pan. Stir remaining ingredients until blended and pour over chicken. Bake at 375° for 40 min. Serve over rice.

Tina with her real life mom, Yvonne & sister Cathy

POPPY SEED CHICKEN
(Phyllis Heim)
A great recipe for a crowd

Serves 12

4 cups chicken, cooked and cut into small pieces
2 cans cream of chicken soup
52 crushed Ritz crackers   ½ cup butter, melted
1 Tbsp. poppy seeds   1 large sour cream

Combine crackers, butter and poppy seeds. Press ½ of cracker mixture on bottom of 9X13 inch baking dish. Mix together chicken, sour cream, and soup. Pour over cracker layer. Sprinkle remaining cracker mixture on top. Bake for 1 hour at 350°. This can be a fairly rich recipe. Calories, salt and fat can be lowered using reduced salt & reduced fat Ritz Crackers, light sour cream, and reduced fat creamed soups.

PSEUDO CHICKEN CORDON BLEU
(Debbie Fox)

Serves 6

6 boneless, skinless chicken breasts   6 slices deli ham
1 can cream of chicken soup   6 slices Swiss cheese
1 cup sour cream

Place chicken in 9x13 pan coated with cooking spray. Lay ham and cheese slices over each piece of chicken. Mix soup and sour cream. Spread over chicken. Bake uncovered for 45 minutes at 375°. Serve with rice or noodles. The sauce is delicious as a gravy.

WHITE CHICKEN CHILI

(Tina Cole, Brooke Smith, Laurette Walton, Debbie Fox)

Every time Tina enters this recipe in a contest, she walks away with 1st or 2nd place! It's got just the right amount of heat.

Serves 10-12

4 cups cooked chicken breasts, in bite-sized pieces
1 bag white beans, or 5 cans of white beans
8 cups chicken broth   2 med. yellow onion, chopped
2 cloves garlic, minced   1 ½ tsp. oregano
1 Tbsp. vegetable oil   2 tsp. cumin
½ tsp. cayenne pepper   3 cups jack cheese, grated
2 (4-oz.) cans chopped green chilies

For those who like more heat, Brooke Smith adds:
8 fresh Anaheim chilies, seeded
1 Tbsp. chili powder
1 Tbsp. hot pepper sauce

Soak dry beans overnight in water. Rinse, drain water, and put in a soup pot with chicken broth, 1 chopped onion, and garlic. Bring to a boil; then simmer for 3 hours. In skillet, sauté oil, 1 chopped onion, chilies, and spices until onion is transparent. Add onion mixture and chicken to beans and simmer another hour.

Before serving, stir in cheese and serve with toppings of your choice:

tortilla chips, salsa, sour cream, lemon and/or lime slices, avocado pieces, black olives, tomatoes, chopped green onion, grated Jack & cheddar cheese

CHICKEN CHOW MEIN

(Donna King Conkling)

Serves 12

3-4 chicken breasts
6 ribs of celery, chopped
1 can sliced water chestnuts
1 can bamboo shoots (optional)
1 green pepper, chopped
1 cup fresh or canned bean sprouts
1 can pineapple tidbits, drained
6 - 8 cups cooked white rice
2 chicken bouillon cubes
1 onion, chopped
Lawry's, pepper
Soy sauce
Bead Molasses syrup
½ cup water
½ cup cornstarch
Chinese fried noodles (canned)

Put chicken in large pot of water with bouillon cubes. Add all vegetables and stew for approximately 30 minutes-1 hour. Cut chicken into bite-size pieces. Add pineapple. Season to taste with Lawry's, pepper, soy sauce and Bead Molasses (if you can find it). Thicken sauce by stirring in a paste made of cornstarch and cold water (add water a little at a time until consistency of heavy cream). Serve over rice with Chinese fried noodles on top.

Donna King Conkling with daughters Xan & Candy

TUSCANY CHICKEN
(Cathy Green)

When we were Italy, we stayed at a lovely farmhouse in Tuscany. A wonderful care-taker and cook named Veronica would go to the village everyday and bring home the freshest ingredients. This is one of our favorites. Simple but delicious.

Serves 6-8

6-8 half-breasts of chicken
1 tsp. salt
4-6 eggs, whipped
½ tsp. pepper
Juice of 1 lemon
4 Tbsp. butter
1 cup grated Parmesan cheese
2 Tbsp. olive oil

Pound each ½ breast until relatively flat. Make a batter of eggs, salt, pepper, and lemon juice. Dip chicken in batter. Lightly coat chicken on both sides with Parmesan cheese. Melt butter and olive oil in large skillet on medium high heat until butter foams. Add chicken breasts and sauté until golden on both sides. Cook well, but don't overcook. It should be tender with a light crust of Parmesan cheese. Serve with penne` pasta topped with tomato or marinara sauce, green vegetables, and Italian salad.

PSEUDO ROTISSERIE CHICKEN

(Carolyn Cameron)

You know the wonderful already cooked whole Rotisserie Chicken that you can buy at the grocery store? I have discovered how to do it at home, on the BBQ.

Makes 1 whole chicken
1 whole fryer chicken

Spices:
½ tsp ea: Lawry's, pepper, thyme, basil, oregano,
or your favorite poultry rub

Buy one of those metal stands that you put a whole chicken on to cook it standing upright. Mix spices together to your liking and taste. Slide your fingers or a butter knife under the skin on both the breast side and the back side of the chicken. Rub the spices all over the chicken under the skin. Place the chicken on the stand. Prepare your BBQ for indirect cooking, which means if it is a gas grill, heat all of the burners on high and then turn off the middle burner(s). The temperature will be about 450°. Place the chicken in a pan on the rack that can go on the grill. The temperature will slowly go down as you lower the remaining burners. You want the temperature to be at about 350° for the rest of the cooking time. Close the lid and let cook for about 1 hour. It is as juicy as the store bought chicken, costs much less, and fun to do.

LEMON MUSTARD MARINADE - FOR CHICKEN
(Brooke Smith)

For 4 chicken breasts

3 Tbsp. Dijon mustard
2 Tbsp. fresh lemon juice
1 tsp. hot sauce (optional)
½ tsp. dried thyme or basil

2 green onions, finely chopped
2 Tbsp. olive oil
1 garlic clove, finely chopped

Stir all ingredients together and set aside ¼ cup of mixture for basting. Marinate 4 chicken breasts in remaining mixture for about 4-6 hours (the longer, the better) in the refrigerator.

PESTO PIZZA
(Laurette Walton)

Serves 8

2 tsp. yeast dissolved with 1 cup lukewarm water
Pesto sauce (homemade or 1 jar store bought)
2-2 ¼ cups flour   Olive oil
Salt and pepper   5-6 Roma tomatoes, sliced
1 ½ cup grated mozzarella cheese
¾ cup Parmesan cheese (or Romano)

Stir water and yeast till dissolved. Add flour and a little salt and mix in bowl. Knead 10 times in bowl. Coat ball of dough in olive oil and let rise 20 minutes. Roll out dough and put in round pizza pan. Add pesto sauce and cover dough as you would pizza sauce. Add lots of sliced Roma tomatoes, salt and pepper. Cover with grated mozzarella cheese and sprinkle with grated Parmesan and/or Romano. Bake 425° for 15-20 minutes.

CHICKEN TETTRAZINI
(Laurette Walton)

Serves 10-12
6 boneless chicken breasts, cooked and cubed
1 lb. cooked spaghetti pasta
1 can cream of mushroom soup
1 can cream of chicken soup
½ lb. fresh mushrooms
2 Tbsp. butter
¼ cup white cooking wine
2 Tbsp. lemon juice
Salt, white pepper, Lawry's
1 pint sour cream
½ tsp. paprika
¾ cup grated Parmesan cheese
1½ tsp. tarragon

Melt butter in fry pan, sauté mushrooms and cook 3-5 minutes. Add lemon juice, white wine and cook a couple more minutes. (If you leave the mushrooms out of the recipe, you still need to melt the butter and cook with lemon and wine because you need the liquid.)

In a LARGE mixing bowl combine 6 cooked boneless, skinless chicken breasts cut up into bite sized pieces, mushroom soup and cream of chicken soup (I use both cream of chicken), sour cream, just a little less than 1 lb. of cooked spaghetti (a full pound can make it seem dry). Add salt, Lawry's and white pepper to taste and tarragon, mushrooms and/or juice. Place in 9x13 pan. Top with grated Parmesan. Bake 325-350° for 30 minutes or until bubbly. Top with paprika for color.

CHICKEN CACCIATORI
(Shauna Elliott)

Serves 3-4

3-4 sliced chicken breasts
1 medium can stewed tomatoes
Spaghetti or any noodles of your choice

3 Tbsp. olive oil   Salt & pepper
Italian seasonings   Garlic to your own taste
2 medium cans tomato sauce

Heat oil and add chicken. Season, cook about 3-5 minutes until done. Remove chicken. Add onion in pan and cook. Stir in garlic 1 minute. Add tomato sauce and stewed tomatoes. Season to taste. Heat and stir for 10 minutes. Simmer 30 minutes. Boil noodles while simmering.

ITALIAN SURPRISE
(Shauna Elliott)

Serves 8-10

1 ½-2 lbs. ground beef, cooked   3 oz. cream cheese
1 pkg. elbow noodles, cooked   1 cup evaporated milk
1-2 cups mozzarella cheese   1 Tbsp. garlic salt
Your own spaghetti sauce (4 or more cups)

In a saucepan melt together the milk, cream cheese and garlic salt. Mix the melted sauce in with the already cooked noodles. Spread on bottom of 9x13 casserole. Brown the beef in a pan; pour in the spaghetti sauce and simmer for 10 min. Pour spaghetti sauce/meat over the noodles and sprinkle with mozzarella cheese. Bake at 350° for ½ hour or if frozen for 1 hour.

OLD WORLD LASAGNA
Candy Brand

After tasting this, you'll never eat frozen Lasagna again!

Serves 9-12

1 lb. ground beef	¼ lb. sausage
1 large can cut up tomatoes	2 (6oz) cans tomato paste
1 clove garlic crushed	½ cup chopped onion
1 Tbsp. oil	1 tsp. dry basil leaves
2 tsp. dry oregano leaves	2 Tbsp. dry parsley
¼ tsp. pepper	1 tsp. salt
2 Tbsp. sugar	1 lb. mozzarella cheese, grated
1 lb. ricotta cheese	1 cup grated Parmesan

1 box lasagna noodles, cooked according to package

Sauté onion in oil, brown beef and sausage and drain oil. Add all other ingredients except cheeses and noodles and simmer 2-3 hours stirring occasionally.

Assemble:
Grease 9x13 Pyrex with butter. Lay four pieces of cooked lasagna to cover bottom, overlapping if necessary. Spread noodles with half the ricotta and mozzarella cheeses. Cover cheeses with half the sauce and sprinkle with half the Parmesan. Repeat. Bake 45-50 minutes in 350°. Let stand 10 to 15 minutes before serving.

CROCKPOT LASAGNA
(Erin Arnett)

Serves 12

¾ pound bulk Italian sausage
12 uncooked lasagna noodles (12 oz.)
1 medium onion, chopped (1/2 cup)
2 (15 oz) cans Italian-style tomato sauce
3 cups (12 oz.) shredded mozzarella cheese
1 container (15 oz.) part-skim ricotta cheese
1 cup grated Parmesan cheese
2 tsp. dried basil leaves
½ tsp. salt

Cook sausage and onion in a skillet over medium heat 6-8 minutes, stirring occasionally, until sausage is no longer pink; drain. Stir in tomato sauce, basil, and salt. Mix 2 cups of the mozzarella cheese and the ricotta and Parmesan cheese. Spoon one-fourth of the sausage mixture into a 3 ½-5-quart slow cooker; top with 4 noodles broken into pieces to fit. Top with half of the cheese mixture and ¼ of the sausage mixture. Top with 4 noodles, remaining cheese mixture and ¼ of the sausage mixture. Top with remaining 4 noodles and remaining sausage mixture. Cover and cook on low heat 6-8 hours or until noodles are tender. Sprinkle top of lasagna with remaining 1 cup mozzarella cheese. Cover and let stand about 10 minutes or until cheese is melted. Cut and serve.

DONNA BELLA À LA FARFELLA

(Candy Brand)

This was created by a local caterer for Donna Conkling's 80th birthday in Roseville, California with the instructions: "For the beautiful Donna; To be cooked for very happy occasions."

Serves 6

3 large chicken breasts	1 cup chicken broth
1 ¼ cups heavy cream	1 Tbsp. olive oil
Bow tie pasta	¼ cup toasted pine nuts
½ cup white flour	1 tsp. minced garlic
¼ tsp. salt	⅛ tsp. pepper
1 Tbsp. butter	1 tsp. dried basil

¼ cup chopped sun dried tomatoes
⅓ cup grated Romano cheese

In food processor, pulse sun dried tomatoes and chicken broth until blended. Toast pine nuts in oven under broiler until just browned. Be careful . . . these burn quickly! Wash chicken, pat dry and cut into bit sized pieces. Toss chicken with flour, salt and pepper. Shake off excess flour. Heat olive oil and butter over medium high heat. Add chicken and brown on all sides. Remove chicken from pan and set aside. Add garlic to pan and sauté for 2 minutes over medium heat. Add chicken broth/sun dried tomato mixture and cook over medium high for a few minutes. Be sure to gently scrape bottom of pan to get loosened browned bits. Add heavy cream, basil, and Romano cheese; reduce heat and simmer for a few minutes. Add chicken and toasted pine nuts and simmer until thickened to desired consistency. Serve over favorite pasta such as farfalle (bow tie pasta).

CHEESE & SPINACH FILLED MANICOTTI
(Lorie Albright)

Serves 8

14 pieces (8 oz.) Manicotti
2 (15 oz.) containers ricotta cheese
2 cups (8oz.) shredded mozzarella
½ cup grated Parmesan
2 eggs
½-1 box frozen spinach, thawed, & drained
2 Tbsp. chopped fresh parsley
½ tsp. salt
¼ tsp. ground black pepper
⅛ tsp. ground nutmeg
14 oz. jar spaghetti sauce

Cook pasta according to package directions and let cool. Mix ricotta cheese, and 1 ½ cups mozzarella and ¼ cup Parmesan cheese with eggs, spinach, parsley and other seasonings. Spoon ½ cup of mixture into each pasta tube. Place stuffed pasta in 9x13 baking pan. Pour sauce over pasta and sprinkle with remaining mozzarella and Parmesan. Cover with foil and bake at 350° for 25 minutes or until hot and bubbly.

MEXICAN CHICKEN CASSEROLE
(Xan Albright)

Serves 9-12

4-6 chicken breasts, stewed (save liquid)
1 (16 oz) jar salsa (mild or medium)
1 pkg. corn tortillas (12)
1 (7 oz.) can diced green chilies
2 cans cream of chicken soup
¼ cup dried onion,
Pepper, Lawry's to taste
2 cups Jack cheese, shredded

Break up tortillas in the bottom of a 9x13 pan and pour a few spoonfuls of chicken broth over to flavor. Break up chicken into bite-sized chunks and spread ½ of chicken over the tortillas. Mix with the rest of the ingredients and pour ½ the mixture over the chicken. Repeat the layers - tortillas (but no more chicken stock on this layer), chicken, and one final cheese layer. Bake 350° for 30-40 minutes. Best to make a day ahead and refrigerate to flavor properly.

The girl cousins singing during the popular "Top Twenty" segment of our 1965-66 TV series "The King Family Show"

MEXICAN LASAGNA
(Shauna Elliott)

Serves 12

2 cups drained cottage cheese
2 lbs. ground beef
1 onion (med.) chopped
2 packets taco seasoning
2 eggs - beaten
6 large flour tortillas
1 ½ cups shredded Jack cheese

Toppings:
shredded lettuce
shredded cheddar cheese
tomatoes – cut
sour cream
black olives avocado slices

Heat oven to 350°. Put cottage cheese into a colander and let it drain in the sink while you brown the beef and onions in a pan. Drain off fat and add taco seasoning, following packet instructions. Mix the cottage cheese, eggs and Monterey jack cheese in a bowl. Line a 9x13 casserole dish with 2 - 3 tortillas. Layer ½ the seasoned beef mix on the tortillas followed by ½ the cheese mixture, then 2 - 3 more tortillas, remaining beef, then remaining cheese mixture. Bake for 30 minutes and let cool for 5 minutes before cutting into squares. Serve on top of shredded lettuce topped with your choice of toppings.

FAJITAS
(Xan Albright)

Serves 8

2 lb. steak or chicken	Tomatoes
2 Tbsp. butter	Red, yellow, green bell peppers
Yellow, red onions	Flour tortillas
Grated cheese	Salsa
Sour cream	Guacamole

Marinade:

1 pkg. Au Jus gravy mix	1 cup water
½ tsp. crushed garlic	3 Tbsp. Worcestershire sauce
3 Tbsp. lime juice	3 Tbsp. peanut oil (optional)

Make marinade, pour over meat, and set in fridge overnight. The next day grill on barbeque (or sauté on stove) and cut up meat. Sauté vegetables in butter until tender, using some of marinade too. Add chopped meat and heat. Serve with flour tortillas, sour cream, guacamole, cheese, and salsa.

Xan at a '60s family picnic

SPINACH FETA PIE
(Chick Rey)

Serves 6-8

12 Filo leaves, purchase at specialty store
2 (10 oz. ea.) boxes frozen chopped spinach
½ lb. feta cheese, crumbled
½ cup butter
2 eggs
1 cup cottage cheese

Place 6 of the Filo leaves on bottom of 2-qt. casserole dish. Melt butter and drip half of melted butter over Filo in casserole. Beat eggs and combine with cottage cheese. Stir in Feta cheese. Cook and drain spinach according to directions on package. Add to cheese and egg mixture. Pour onto Filo leaves in baking dish. Top with remaining Filo leaves and drip with remaining melted butter. Bake at 350° for 40 min.

CROCKPOT TACO CASSEROLE
(Erin Arnett)
A great dinner for busy, working Moms!

Serves 6-8

1 ½ lbs. ground hamburger, browned
1 can (14 oz.) diced tomatoes w/green chilies
1 can (10 oz.) cream of chicken soup
1 Tbsp. dried onion   1 pkg. taco seasoning
¼ cup water   6 corn tortillas cut in strips
½ cup sour cream   1 cup shredded cheese

Cook first 7 ingredients in a slow cooker, 3-5 hours. Has the consistency of almost a bean/cheese dip. Delicious! Serve by spreading sour cream over it and sprinkle with cheese.

ENCHILADAS VERDES
(Wendy Moran)

Serves 5-6
3 lbs. chicken, cooked and shredded
10-12 large flour tortillas
2 ½ cups cheddar cheese, grated

Sauce:
2 lbs. tomatillos
1 clove garlic
Cilantro to taste
1 ½ cups chopped onion
2-5 Serrano chilies (depending on how hot you like it)
1 cup sour cream

Remove tomatillos from skins and wash well and place in a large pot of boiling water with Serrano chilies. Boil for five min., drain. Blend tomatillos, chilies, garlic and cilantro in a blender until smooth. Pour into medium bowl; mix in onions and sour cream. Place some chicken and 2 - 3 Tbsp. sauce (you should not use all the sauce inside the enchiladas) and a little cheese on a tortilla and roll and place in a 9x13 Pyrex. Squeeze in 10 - 12 filled tortillas. Pour remaining sauce over enchiladas and top with remaining cheese. Bake at 350° for 30 minutes. Serve with rice and beans.

CHICK'S CHILI RELLENOS
(Chick Rey)

Makes 6

Sauce:
1 large can tomato juice
1 bay leaf (discard when cooked)
1 bouillon cube
Dash onion salt
Dash garlic salt
2 sprigs fresh cilantro
Bring sauce ingredients to boil and keep hot.

Chilies:
6 green chili peppers, preferably Anaheim; remove seeds
6 (1½" x ½") squares of Monterey Jack cheese
Peanut oil for deep frying
Wrap each chili around a square of cheese.

Batter:
6 eggs, separated   6 Tbsp. flour   1 tsp. salt

Beat yolks separately, until light yellow and thick; mix in ½ tsp. salt. In a separate bowl, beat egg whites and ½ tsp. salt until stiff but not dry. Fold yolks into whites. Then fold flour into egg mixture, using wire whisk. Do this folding very gently.

To assemble: Heat peanut oil, enough to cover the chilies, in a deep kettle. Dip wrapped chilies into egg batter, making sure they are covered with batter. Lift them out with a spoon and fry in hot oil until brown on one side. Baste before turning, to keep them from coming apart and splattering. Use a spoon and pancake turner to turn them. They may have to be turned once again. When light brown remove and drain on paper towel. Just before serving, immerse the chilies in the hot tomato sauce and serve immediately with additional sauce if desired. Garnish with grated cheese, chopped cilantro, green onions, and parsley.

CHILI & BEANS
(Marilyn King, Alyce King Clarke)

Linda de Azevedo remembers Alyce serving this on a cold (relatively speaking) California December night while Bob, Ric, Lex and Cam strung the Christmas lights on the old homestead in Studio City, California. In the summer, serve it with coleslaw and grilled sourdough bread. Some like mixing the coleslaw in with the chili.

Serves 12-16
2 cans whole Ortega chilies, seeded and sliced (not chopped)
2 cans Las Palmas enchilada sauce
2 lb. hamburger
2 chopped onions
6 large cans red kidney beans

Serve with:
Chopped onion	Grated cheese	Sour cream
Black olives	Lawry's, pepper	

Simmer together chilies and enchilada sauce. In a large kettle, brown hamburger and onion, drain. Add kidney beans and use most of the liquid (save some for later in case you need more liquid). Stir in chili/enchilada sauce. Add more bean juice if needed as you cook. Season to taste. Serve with chopped onion, grated cheese, sour cream, and black olives.

SAUSAGE CASSEROLE
(Laurette Walton)
A little different but so delicious!

Serves 12

1 ½ lbs. pork sausage (I use 1lb. hot, ½ lb. mild)
2 pkgs. Lipton Chicken Noodle Soup Mix (with chicken)
2 Tbsp. butter or margarine
1 green pepper, diced
3 stalks celery, diced
4 ½ cups boiling water
1 medium onion, diced
1 cup uncooked white rice
½ cup slivered or sliced almonds:
  (cooked for a few minutes in fry pan with a little butter)

Brown sausage and drain. Cook veggies in butter until soft. Boil the water. Dissolve soup in the boiling water. Stir rice, veggies, and sausage into the water. Pour into either 9x13 Pyrex or deep covered round casserole dish. Bake covered (you can use foil) at 350° for 40 minutes. Then bake uncovered for 15-20 minutes more. Sprinkle with almonds for the last 5 minutes.

Donna King Conkling with her daughter Laurette

ST. PATRICK'S DAY CORN BEEF AND CABBAGE
(Donna King Conkling)

The King Sister's always had a St. Patrick's Party and served this traditional dish along with Irish soda bread.

Serves 6-8

1 corned beef roast
Head of green cabbage, cut into quarters
6 medium potatoes peeled
6-8 carrots sliced
2 onions, quartered
Lawry's, pepper
1 cup mayonnaise
⅓ cup mustard

Cook corned beef according to the package directions included with the meat. In a separate kettle, partially boil all the vegetables. Towards the end of cooking the meat, place the underdone vegetables in with the meat until all are cooked well. Salt and pepper to taste. Serve on a platter with the vegetables around the meat. Mix mayo and mustard to make mustard sauce as garnish. Serve with Irish soda bread and "Pear Lime Jell-O". (see Index)

Donna & Jim Conkling at a '60s family party

TWICE BAKED POTATOES WITH HAM
(Erin Arnett)
Along with a salad, this is all you need for a great dinner!

Serves 12-14
8 potatoes
1 cup cooked chopped ham (bacon is good also)
1 cup sour cream (½ cup of milk can be used)
1 cup cubed medium sharp cheese
¼ cup butter
Lawry's, pepper
Paprika

Bake 8 potatoes about 1 hour at 425°. When baked, cut in half lengthwise. Scoop out potatoes and put in mixing bowl. Save potato skins. Mix all other ingredients together well and add seasoning to taste. Return potato mixture to potato skin halves, piling high. Sprinkle with a small amount of paprika for color. Bake again for 15 minutes at 300° or heat under broiler for a few seconds. Serve with a green salad.

Alvino Rey & the Cousins performing on "The King Family Show"

HAM SOUFFLÉ
(Alyce King Clarke)
Light and fluffy and a great dish for your leftover ham.

Serves 10-12

2 cups ground ham (use a grinder or a food processor)
4 Tbsp. flour   4 Tbsp. butter
2 cups milk   3 eggs, separated
2 - 3 cups cheese, grated

Make a white sauce by stirring in flour to melted butter. Add milk, stirring till it boils and thickens. Add ham and cheese and stir until it melts. Let cool. Beat 3 egg whites stiff and beat 3 yolks. Stir the egg yolks into the cooled mixture; then carefully fold in the egg whites. Pour into 9X13 (or slightly smaller) Pyrex. Place this pan in a larger pan and fill that larger one with 1"of water. Bake at 350° for 1 hour.

LEFTOVER HAM CASSEROLE
(Carolyn Cameron)

Serves 8-10

2 cups ham, chopped
1 cup butter   1 ½-2 cups rice, already cooked
2 Tbsp. parsley   1 Tbsp. pepper
Lawry's only if needed (ham is very salty already)
1 cup each: celery, carrots, green peppers, onion, all chopped

Sauté chopped celery, carrots, green bell peppers and onion in butter in medium kettle. Add ham and warm through. Pour all into a 9X13 Pyrex over the rice and mix thoroughly. Season to taste. This is a great comfort food for me.

POACHED SALMON
(Yvonne King Burch)

Finally, a fabulous fish recipe that doesn't make your house smell. This can be served as a main dish but also makes a delicious base for salmon tacos.

Serves 4-6

2-3 lb. fresh salmon, Columbia or Alaskan
Juice of 2 lemons   2 Tbsp. honey
2 onion slices   1 tsp. Lawry's
1 liter lemon-lime soda

Make marinade with lemon juice, honey, onions and Lawry's. Cover salmon in marinade for 1 hour. Place the salmon in 9X13 Pyrex. Add enough lemon/lime soda to cover it. Bake 350° for 30 - 45 min. Serve with asparagus and red potatoes. Serve hollandaise sauce over asparagus and the salmon. To serve the salmon, turn it over and remove the brownish skin from the bottom of the salmon, so there shouldn't be skin on either side of the salmon. You can use this recipe with white fish too (halibut, sole), but cover with milk instead of 7-UP.

**Vonnie on the set of our TV series "The King Family Show"
Note the beautiful Bob Mackie designed gown she's wearing**

FRESH BARBECUED TROUT
Liza Rey

1 fresh, whole trout	1 lemon slices
2 springs fresh dill	2 bacon slices

Use fresh, cleaned trout (cut out gills, but leave the head on). Place fresh dill and a lemon slice inside. Wrap bacon around the trout, securing with a toothpick. Place trout in a barbecue square holder and cook about 4-5 min. each side until browned.

Alvino Rey with two of his kids - Liza & Rob

PAELLA
(Liza Rey)

Serves 4

8 chicken thighs or legs or combo
14 oz. can diced tomatoes
2 cups brown rice, uncooked
1 cup green pepper, chopped
1 tsp. onion powder
1 tsp. garlic powder
¼ cup butter
1 tsp. saffron
3 cups chicken broth
1 cup white wine
½ cup frozen peas

Fry chicken and cut into pieces. Sauté onion powder and garlic powder and green pepper in butter. Add saffron to add yellow color and the tomatoes. In a separate pan cook brown rice for the length of time on the box, using the broth and wine as the liquid. Add the sautéed mixture. The rice will be juicy. Place the rice mixture in a "paella pan" (a low, flat pan) and artistically arrange the chicken on the rice. You may need to add more liquid broth. You may freeze the rice/chicken mixture and simply add the fresh fish before cooking, if you want. Artistically arrange the uncooked clams and mussels around the chicken. Scatter frozen peas around. Cover in foil, and cook at 350° for 45 min., until the shellfish is cooked. Serve with sourdough bread.

DALE'S BBQ SHRIMP CREOLE STYLE
(Dale Foshée)

Serves 6-8

2½ lbs. of jumbo shrimp (deveined/ tail on)
1 large or 2 small yellow onions broken up by hand
Steamed rice for 6-8
1-3 Tbsp. olive oil
8 cloves of garlic
3 sticks of butter
1 Tbsp. chili powder
1 Tbsp. paprika
6 Tbsp. Tabasco sauce
¼ tsp. cayenne pepper
1 tsp. of Tony Chachere's Creole Seasoning
½ tsp. pepper
Juice of 4 lemons
¼ cup white wine
1 bunch of cilantro, chopped 3 lemons, sliced
½ cup heavy cream (add more to soften taste if needed)

Coat a large skillet or wok with olive oil. Add onions and garlic; brown a bit. Add the butter and all the dry ingredients plus the lemon juice. Stir on medium high until bubbly. Add the shrimp and continue stirring as needed, 7 min. or so. Add the wine as needed to steam and keep from drying out. Add cilantro the last few minutes and the cream at the end. Stir the cream for 2-3 min; add the lemon slices and stir a minute or so. Pour over the steamed rice. So great!

Soups

Marilyn King performing on "The King Family Show" 1965

POTATO CHICKEN POTAGE
(Marilyn King)

Serves 8-10
3 chicken breasts, cooked and cut into small pieces
5 ribs celery, chopped
½ cup green onion, chopped
3 Tbsp. butter

In a large pot sauté celery and green onion in butter until tender. Add chicken and homemade or canned potato soup.

Soup:
Honestly, the addition of chicken and green vegetables is a good way to "doctor" a canned potato soup (probably 2 - 3 cans) if you're in a hurry OR make soup below:

10 oz. can cream of chicken soup
3-4 cups Half & Half
2 lbs. frozen hash browns, thawed
1 cup shredded cheddar cheese
Lawry's and pepper, to taste

Heat soup, Half & Half, and potatoes. Stir in cheese; add chicken pieces and sautéed onion and celery. Season as needed.

NAVY BEAN SOUP
(Grandma Pearl Driggs)

On a cold, "Southern California winter" night, Grandma Pearl's old-fashioned comfort food created the cozy background for many casual family get-togethers.

Serves 8

Ham pieces or ham hock
1 lb. navy beans
1 medium chopped onion
Lawry's and pepper to taste

Soak the beans overnight. In the morning drain water, throwing away any rocks. Cook all ingredients in a large pot in enough water to cover them. Bring to boil and simmer, covered for 2-4 hours. No better simple recipe than this.

TOMATO CLAM BISQUE
(Phyllis Heim)

Serves 8

4 cans of clams, chopped or minced
Clam juice (from the clams) to taste
4 cans tomato soup
1 can chicken broth
3 cans milk (can substitute some cream for a richer soup)
Cayenne pepper – a dash
1 bunch green onions, chopped
White pepper, to taste

Put all ingredients in a large pot. Simmer but do not boil for at least one hour.

TORTILLA SOUP CROCKPOT
(Candy Brand)

Serves 16

1 ½ lbs. boneless chicken cooked and shredded
1 can (15 oz.) whole tomatoes chopped
1 can (10 oz.) enchilada sauce
2 cans (14 oz.) chicken broth
1 can (4 oz.) diced green chilies
1 medium onion, chopped
1 clove garlic, minced
1 pkg. frozen corn
1 cup water
1 tsp. Chili powder
1 tsp. cumin
1 tsp. Salt
¼ tsp. pepper
1 Bay leaf
1 Tbsp. cilantro

Serve with:
Tortilla chips
Grated cheese
Diced avocados
Sour cream

In crockpot combine all ingredients except chicken and cilantro. Cook on low 6-8 hours or 3-4 hours on high. Add chicken and cilantro the last ½ hour to heat. Serve soup with diced avocados, sour cream, tortilla chips and grated cheese as condiments on top.

CREAM OF CHICKEN SOUP

(Candy Brand, Noelle Sanderson)
Great for an easy Christmas Eve dinner!

Serves 8-10

3 chicken breasts (stewed – retain the broth)
2 cups finely chopped onion
2 cups diced potatoes
1 cup diced celery
¾ cup flour
1 ½ tsp. sugar
¾ cup butter
1 quart Half & Half
Lawry's, pepper

Cook veggies in Crockpot covered with broth from chicken and enough water to cover. Cook low for 5 hours. Make a white sauce: Melt butter and mix with flour – blend with wire whisk. Gradually add Half & Half and sugar and whisk together over low heat until thickened and smooth. Add white sauce and cut up chicken to veggie mixture (do not drain the broth and water) and cook 1 more hour. Add milk if it gets too thick. Season with Lawry's and pepper to taste. Note: This can also be made in a large pot on the stove: over low heat, simmer veggies for 30 min. Make white sauce as instructed above. Combine all ingredients and simmer another 30 min.

King Sister Alyce with cousins Jamie, Chris, Candy, Xan, Cathy, Carolyn & Tina riding in the Hollywood Christmas Parade

BROCCOLI CHEESE SOUP
(Laurette Walton)

Serves 8-10
2 cups finely chopped broccoli (fresh)
1 ½ -2 cups cubed Velveeta cheese
6 cups chicken broth
3-4 med. carrots, grated
½ cup butter
1 cup flour
Salt, pepper to taste

In a large pot, steam veggies until crisp but tender. Set aside. Melt butter. Add flour and make a roux cooking over medium heat a few minutes. Do not burn. Add broth, blending over low heat until smooth. After it thickens a bit and is bubbly, add cheese cubes and stir until melted (if it isn't cheesy enough add more to taste). You can also add salt and pepper to taste. Add steamed veggies and cook till heated through.

King Kids Laurette, Cam & Susannah on "The King Family Show"

MINESTRONE SOUP

(Yvonne King Burch)

Vonnie, a wonderful gourmet cook, can also respect a "semi-homemade" method to create a recipe fabulous enough to serve company.

Serves 8-10

1 lb. stewing meat, floured
½ cup sherry wine or cooking sherry
1 large can Progresso minestrone soup
2 cans Italian style tomatoes w/ basil
Small package bowtie pasta
1 can white beans
2 tsp. anise
2 zucchinis, quartered
Juice of 1 - 2 lemons
1 onion, chopped
Oregano or tarragon, to taste

Brown meat that's been floured. Cover in water. Add onion, cover, and simmer for several hours in a kettle. Add remaining ingredients (except for the lemon juice and pasta), and cook another hour. Add lemon juice and pasta the last 15 minutes. You can also add any leftover vegetables you have in the fridge. Serve with a beautiful salad and gorgeous bread.

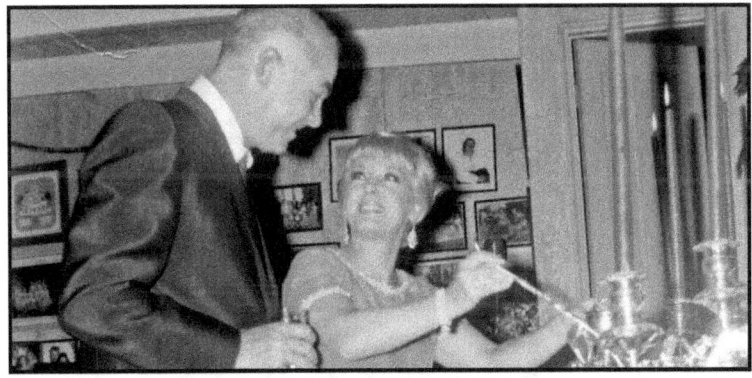

Vonnie & husband Bill Burch

CHEESY HAM CHOWDER WITH VEGETABLES
(Xan Albright)

Serves 8

2 cups cooked ham, cubed
2 cups water
1 ½ cups chopped potatoes
2 cups milk
¾ cup chopped carrots
2½ cups shredded cheese
1 (15 oz.) can creamed corn
½ cup chopped celery
¼ cup chopped onion
¼ cup flour
¼ cup butter
½ tsp pepper

Cover the vegetables with the water in a pot. Boil and simmer, covered, 20 min. Make the cheese sauce in a separate pot: Melt butter and stir in flour and pepper. Add milk and cook until thickened and bubbly. Add cheese to the sauce and stir till melted. Add the sauce to the vegetables. Stir in ham and corn and heat but do not boil.

Candy, Tina & Xan on "The King Family Show"

GREEK LEMON RICE SOUP
(Chick Rey)

Serves 6-8

3 (15 oz.) cans chicken broth
⅓ cup uncooked rice
¼ cup lemon juice
2 cups water
3 eggs

Heat broth and water in a saucepan to boiling; add rice. Reduce heat; cover and simmer until rice is tender, about 15 minutes. Remove from heat. In a bowl, beat eggs with a rotary beater until fluffy. Slowly beat lemon juice into eggs, then gradually beat in 1 cup of the broth mixture. Stirring constantly, slowly add egg mixture to remaining hot broth in pan. Chill if making ahead. Just before serving, heat soup until hot. DO NOT BOIL. Serve with a sprig of parsley and a slice of lemon.

TORTELLINI SOUP
(Jamie Miller)

Serves 8

3 (10 oz.) cans chicken broth
1 (14 oz.) jar tomato and basil pasta sauce
1 pkg. baby carrots (whole or sliced)
1 tsp. Italian herb seasoning
3 medium zucchini, sliced
1 pkg. cheese tortellini (you can use fresh or the dried)
Parmesan cheese

Bring first 4 ingredients to a boil and simmer 20 minutes or until done. Add zucchini and tortellini. Cook for another 20 minutes or until done. Sprinkle with Parmesan cheese.

TINA'S NORWEGIAN CAULIFLOWER SOUP
(Tina Cole)
Even if you hate cauliflower, you'll love this

Serves 6

1 med. head cauliflower
3 cans of cream of chicken soup
3 soup cans full of Half & Half
1 Tbsp. chicken bouillon granules
3 pieces of celery, chopped
½ yellow onion, chopped
10 slices bacon
2 Tbsp. butter
Grated nutmeg

Boil cauliflower in salted water (not mushy). Save water and cut cauliflower in bite-sized florets and set aside. Fry bacon in large skillet until crisp. Put on paper towel, crumble, and set aside. Pour off fat, leaving about ¼ cup. Add butter to bacon fat and sauté onion and celery until tender. Sprinkle with bouillon granules, stirring to blend. Pour soup mixture into skillet and stir until smooth. Add cauliflower and bacon and blend. Simmer; do not boil, for 5 minutes. Best made a day in advance. Serve, sprinkle with nutmeg.

**The Four King Cousins from the 1969 TV Special
"Holiday Cruise with the King Family"**

SANTA ANA ALBONDIGAS SOUP
(Carolyn Cameron)

Serves 12

1 cup chopped onion
1 tsp. basil
1 Tbsp. butter
1 tsp. oregano
4 cups water
½ cup rice (uncooked)
5 (10 ½ oz) cans beef bouillon
2 (7 oz.) cans green chili salsa
1 (28 oz) can diced tomatoes
Cornmeal meatballs (see recipe below)

In large pot, sauté onions in butter and add all the other ingredients except meatballs and rice. Bring to a boil and simmer 20 minutes. While simmering, make meatballs:

Cornmeal Meatballs:
2 Tbsp. olive oil
½ lbs ground chuck   ¼ tsp pepper
¼ lb ground pork   ¼ tsp garlic powder
1 onion, chopped   ¼ tsp basil
1 egg, beaten   ¼ c. milk
½ tsp salt   ½ cup cornmeal

Combine all ingredients; form into balls, and brown in olive oil. Add rice and meatballs to soup and simmer for 1½ hours. You can add a little sour cream and chives to each serving as garnish if desired. It's a full meal.

Salads & Dressings

Alvino Rey & The King Sisters (Luise, Alyce, Vonnie & Marilyn)
circa 1965

DONNA'S POTATO SALAD

(Donna King Conkling)

Served at every King Family picnic! There are many varieties of potato salad, but the King Family's loyalty is to this recipe. It conjures up memories of family and games and togetherness and glorious food sitting out for hours for people to enjoy on a warm, California summer day – before we worried about things like mayonnaise spoiling & food poisoning!

A favorite King Family picnic game was called New Orleans. Here's how we played it: Divide the group into 2 teams. Each team secretly decides on a movie, book, or song title to act out. Teams line up shoulder-to-shoulder facing the opposing team (on a marked or imaginary "starting line"), who stand shoulder-to-shoulder about 30-40 feet away on their "line." The 2 teams walk slowly toward each other, shouting the following chant, eventually meeting in the middle (leaving about 6 - 8 feet between the two teams):

Team 1:	Here we come.
Team 2:	Where from?
Team 1:	New Orleans.
Team 2:	What's your trade?
Team 1:	Lemonade.
Team 2:	Show us if you're not afraid!

Team 1: Performs group "charade" (i.e., Some Like it Hot, Star Wars, Finding Nemo, Surfin' Safari, Animal Farm)

Team 2: Shouts out answers and when someone guesses the right title, Team 1 starts running back to their starting line. Team 2 chases after them and tries to tag anyone on Team 1. Anyone they tag now becomes a member of Team 2, and the play continues as before. Game is over when everyone ends up on one side.

Serves 12-15

10 potatoes (white rose)
12 eggs, hard boiled
Lawry's
1 quart mayonnaise
1-2 Tbsp. onion, finely chopped
Pepper to taste
Paprika

Boil potatoes in jackets. Peel and slice. Add a LOT of Lawry's and let it "season" one hour in fridge. When cooled, mix together the onion and 9 of the hard boiled eggs in a large bowl. Then add LOADS of mayonnaise and more Lawry's. Slice remaining hard boiled eggs decoratively around top of salad. Sprinkle paprika on the top. Donna says the more mayo the better!!!!

1941 ad featuring Alvino & The King Sisters (Yvonne, Donna, Luise & Alyce - before Marilyn took over for sister Donna)

RASPBERRY/BLUEBERRY GREEN SALAD
(Candy Brand, Brooke Smith, Noelle Sanderson)

Serves:
Any amount, depending on how much of each you use.
Mixed Greens
Raspberries
Blueberries
Chopped red onion
Gorgonzola cheese
Candied Pecans

Dressing:
¾ cup vegetable oil
2 cloves minced garlic
¾ cup sugar
½ tsp. salt
½ cup red wine vinegar
½ tsp. paprika
¼ tsp. pepper

Make dressing ahead and refrigerate to "season." Toss salad with dressing.

Tina, Candy, Carolyn, Cathy & Jamie on the 1969 TV Special "June with the King Family"

VEGETABLE SALAD
(Yvonne King Burch)

Serves 8

1 red onion, cut in small wedges
2 cups red cabbage   2 cups green cabbage
½ box frozen petite peas   1 can corn

Dressing:
⅓ cup Oil and ¼ cup vinegar
2-4 Tbsp. mayonnaise
1 tsp. sugar
Lawry's

Mix dressing together and pour over salad ingredients. Put in the peas still frozen as it only takes a minute to thaw them. Use red onion in small wedges.

FETA SALAD
(Chick Rey)

Serves 4-6

Salad:
Lettuce (romaine, chicory, bib and Boston)
1 cup Feta cheese, crumbled
Greek olives, as desired

Dressing:
½ cup olive oil   ¼ cup vinegar
1 tsp. garlic powder   1 tsp. onion powder
Lawry's, Pepper to taste

Combine dressing ingredients (can include a dash of oregano). Tear lettuce into large bowl. Break in Feta cheese; add Greek olives. Toss the salad with dressing.

BROCCOLI SALAD
(Donna King Conkling, Carolyn Cameron)

Serves 8-10

1 pkg. frozen broccoli florets (thawed)
   or 1 lb. fresh broccoli (chopped)
1 cup chopped dates   1 cup peanuts or cashews
1 lb. crisp bacon   1 cup white raisins (optional)

Dressing:
⅓ cup sugar   2 Tbsp. vinegar
1 cup mayonnaise   2 Tbsp. frozen orange juice (undiluted)

Toss all ingredients with the dressing and refrigerate. Best served very cold.

PEACH/GRAPE SALAD
(Donna King Conkling and Yvonne King Burch)
It wasn't considered summer until the family had served this.

Serves 8

4 fresh peaches
8 oz. cream cheese, softened and thinned a bit with milk
1 bunch green grapes, each grape cut in half

Take the skin off fresh peaches. Remove pit and cut in half. Dilute cream cheese with milk to the consistency of thick icing. Lay peach half, round side up on a bed of lettuce. "Frost" the rounded side of the peach with the cream cheese (it looks like an igloo). Place green grapes halves, flat side down, over the entire cream cheese peach. This is a delightful and fresh summer salad but it takes awhile to assemble. Make ahead and refrigerate.

HOLIDAY JELL-O SALAD

(Laurette Walton)
Good for kids who "don't like nuts!"

Serves 12-15
2 small pkgs. cherry Jell-O
2 small pkgs. lime Jell-O
1 small pkg. lemon Jell-O
8 oz. softened cream cheese
1 cup mayonnaise
1 cup miniature marshmallows
2 cups crushed pineapple, drained
1 cup heavy cream, whipped and unsweetened

Layer One:
Make lime Jell-O with a little less than 4 cups water. Let set in one size larger than 9x13. If using a 9x13, you will have to discard some of each layer or it will overflow.

Layer Two:
Add 1 cup hot water to lemon Jell-O. Add marshmallows. Heat in saucepan on low till marshmallows are dissolved. Cool slightly. Beat in cream cheese till smooth. Add mayonnaise, crushed pineapple. Fold in whipped cream (measure after whipped and unsweetened). Pour over set lime Jell-O. Let Layer Two set in refrigerator.

Layer Three:
Make cherry Jell-O with just less than 4 cups water. Pour over set white layer. Set till firm.

PEAR LIME JELL-O
(Donna King Conkling)

Serves 6-8

1 large pkg. lime Jell-O
3 ounce package cream cheese
1 can of pears halves
whole walnuts

Prepare lime Jell-O according to package, using pear juice for part of the cold water measurement, and put in an 8X8 pan. Refrigerate until soupy. Meanwhile, place a dob of cream cheese inside the round core of each pear half. Place a walnut on top of cream cheese. When soupy, place the pears in the Jell-O, walnut side down and return to refrigerator until molded. Serve in squares with a pear half in each square. Optional—if you believe in Donna's "more is better" philosophy, add a dollop of sour cream or mayonnaise at the top of each square!

SPINACH CRAISIN SALAD
(Erin Arnett)

Serves 6-8

12 oz. fresh spinach
½ cup Craisins
¼ - ½ small red onion, thinly sliced
½ cup crumbled blue cheese
2 Tbsp. toasted sliced almonds
Dressing:
½ cup bottled balsamic vinaigrette salad dressing
2 Tbsp. orange juice
1 tsp. orange zest

Wash and clean spinach. Tear into bit size pieces and place in a serving bowl. Add onion and half of the feta or goat cheese; toss to combine. Combine dressing ingredients in a small mixing bowl. Pour over salad and toss to coat. Sprinkle with remaining cheese. Top with sweetened Craisins and almonds.

ORANGE - GRAPEFRUIT SALAD WITH HONEY DRESSING
(Phyllis Heim)

Serves 6-8

4 oranges
1 head red leaf lettuce
½ red onion, thinly sliced
2 grapefruits
2 avocado, peeled, sliced

Honey Dressing:
2 Tbsp. fresh parsley leaves (1-2 tsp. if using dry)
1 small onion, chopped
½ tsp. paprika
3 Tbsp. honey
3 Tbsp. cider vinegar
½ tsp. dry mustard
½ tsp. celery seed
1 Tbsp. fresh lemon juice
⅓ cup light oil (preferably Canola)

With a sharp knife, peel oranges and grapefruit – remove white membranes. Cut each in sections. Arrange lettuce in a large circle on a round plate. Arrange orange and grapefruit on lettuce. Peel and slice avocado (squeeze lemon juice on avocado to keep it from turning brown) and arrange in center of plate within circle of fruit slices. Scatter very thinly sliced onion rounds over fruit.

Dressing:
Add parsley and onion to bowl of food processor. Process by turning on/off about 6 times or until finely chopped. Add remaining ingredients and process 10 seconds. Be careful of the amount of onion – it can easily be too strong.

STEAK SUPPER SALAD
(Laurette Walton)

Serves 6

½ head each: Romaine and red leaf lettuce
1 flank steak, 1½ -2 lbs.
1 lb. fresh asparagus
¼ cup olive oil
1 lb. fresh green beans, trimmed
½ cup red wine vinegar
1 red pepper, cut in strips
Pepper to taste
2 lbs. small red potatoes

Dressing:
1 ½ Tbsp. Dijon mustard
Salt & pepper to taste
¼ cup white or red wine vinegar
½ cup olive oil

Marinate steak in the olive oil mixed with vinegar and pepper for 3-4 hours or overnight. Fry the steak in a pan over high heat until medium rare. Cool and cut into julienne strips. Boil potatoes until just tender. Cool and slice. Snap off the tough ends of the asparagus and cook the stalks in a pot of boiling water until tender, then take out and place the green beans in the water to cook until tender. Place both beans and asparagus into ice cold water to stop cooking. Cut the asparagus and beans into 2-inch diagonal pieces. Whisk dressing ingredients. Combine beef, vegetables, bell pepper, dressing and toss. Serve cold on a bed of romaine and leaf lettuce.

FROZEN FRUIT SALAD
(Carolyn Cameron)
Wonderful holiday tradition

Serves approximately 20
8 oz. cream cheese
1 large can crushed pineapple (including juice)
6-7 bananas, sliced in 4th lengthwise and then cubed
1 large can fruit cocktail, drained
1 large bottle maraschino cherries, drained and halved
1 pkg. colored miniature marshmallows
1 pint heavy cream, whipped but not sweetened

Cream the pineapple and cream cheese together in large bowl with electric mixer. Add the bananas, fruit cocktail and cherries to the cream cheese mixture and mix well by hand. Stir in the marshmallows. Whip cream and fold into fruit mixture. Freeze in bread pans for at least 12 hours. Take out of freezer and let stand for about 5 minutes. Slice and serve immediately. To loosen from pan, dip pan in hot water for a few seconds. I slice it with an electric knife. Fills 5 or 6 small loaf pans or 3 large loaf pans.

The Four King Cousins (Cathy, Tina, Candy & Carolyn) backstage at "The Jonathan Winters Show" 1968

BOW TIE CHICKEN SALAD
(Laurette Walton)

Serves 8-10

1 lb. bow tie pasta
15 oz. baby spinach
6 oz. pkg of Craisins
3 (11 Oz) cans of mandarin oranges
2 (8 oz) cans water chestnuts, chopped
2 cups cooked chicken, cubed
6 oz. pkg. honey roasted nuts
Dressing:
⅔ cup white or red wine vinegar
⅔ cup teriyaki sauce
1 cup oil
6 Tbsp. sugar
½ tsp. salt
½ tsp. pepper

Cook bow tie pasta according to package. Mix dressing in blender and marinate pasta in the dressing for 2 hours. Add baby spinach, "Craisins" (little dried cranberries), mandarin oranges, water chestnuts, and chicken. Mix all together with pasta and top with honey roasted nuts.

King Kids Adam, Cam, Susannah, Laurette and Stevo backstage at "The King Family Show" 1965

CHICKEN SALAD
(Candy Brand)

Serves 8

2 cups chicken, cooked and diced
1 cup celery, chopped
1 tsp. freshly ground pepper
¾ cup grapes, halved
1 Tbsp. fresh lemon juice
2 Tbsp. dried dill weed

Dressing:
¼ cup heavy cream, slightly whipped
½ cup mayonnaise
½ cup sliced almonds, toasted

Mix the above ingredients and chill at least 1 hour. Mix all ingredients of the salad together. Toss with dressing and chill for at least 1 hour. Serve on a bed of lettuce. May garnish with quartered hard boiled eggs, tomato wedges, and slices of black olives.

CHINESE CHICKEN SALAD
(Carolyn Cameron)

Serves 6

3 hard boiled eggs, chopped
1 cup Chinese dried noodles
1 can sliced water chestnuts
4 green onions, chopped
2 celery stalks
6 chicken breasts
1 cup grapes, cut in half
½ cup cashews
French dressing
Mayonnaise, to taste

Boil chicken till done. Cool and cut into small pieces. Put in bowl and cover lightly with French dressing. Chill in fridge for several hours. In a large bowl, combine chicken with celery, onions, and water chestnuts. To serve add a little mayo, cashews, grapes, and coarsely chopped eggs. Serve on lettuce and garnish with Chinese noodles.

CHINESE CABBAGE SALAD
(Xan Albright)

Serves 10

1 bag cabbage/slaw mix
1 pkg. Ramen chicken flavored noodles, uncooked and crunched up in bite-size pieces
1 bunch green onions, sliced
3 Tbsp. sunflower seeds (shelled)
Sliced almonds, toasted

Dressing:
½ cup oil   3 Tbsp. red wine vinegar
3 Tbsp. sugar   Flavor packet from Ramen noodles

Combine dressing and put in fridge to chill. Toss dressing with all ingredients.

ARUGULA ORZO SALAD
(Stefanie Heaton)

Serves 8

½ lb. orzo pasta   12 fresh basil leaves, cut
3 Tbsp. olive oil + ¼ cup   ¼ cup toasted pine nuts
½ cup feta cheese   3 Tbsp. lemon juice
½ cup dried cherries   Salt & pepper to taste
2 cups fresh arugula or mixed greens w/ arugula

Cook pasta according to pkg. directions. Drain and spread on cookie sheet to cool, drizzling with olive oil to keep pasta from clumping. Once cool, mix the orzo with remaining ingredients in a large bowl. Toss with remaining ¼ cup of olive oil – no other dressing needed.

PASTA SALAD ORIENTAL
(Debbie Fox)

Serves 8

3 cups cooked chicken, cut into small pieces
1 pkg. bowtie pasta – cooked according to package
½ cup slivered almonds
½ cup parsley, chopped
½ cup green onion, chopped
3 cups torn spinach leaves
½ cup toasted sesame seeds

Dressing: Combine all and set aside.
⅓ cup oil
2 Tbsp. sugar
2 Tbsp. sesame oil
½ tsp. salt
¼ cup soy sauce
½ tsp. pepper
¼ cup rice vinegar
1 tsp. ginger

Combine chicken with salad ingredients and add dressing. Refrigerate 30 minutes.

Susannah, Laurette and Debbie perform "Hey, You Beautiful Doll" on a holiday episode of "The King Family Show" 1965

WINTER SALAD WITH PEARS AND TOASTED PECANS

(Laurette Walton)

Very nice at Thanksgiving or Christmas

Serves 10-12

3 Tbsp. red wine vinegar

2 tsp. Dijon mustard

½ tsp. salt

½ tsp. pepper

⅓ cup oil

Fresh Parmesan cheese

3 medium pears - peeled, cored and cut into thin wedges

Soft lettuce like red leaf or butter lettuce

½ cup pecan halves cooked for a few minutes in butter

In bowl, whisk vinegar, mustard, salt and pepper. Gradually add oil until blended. Add pear wedges and coat with dressing. Add lettuce, Parmesan cheese, and pecans.

A Christmas episode of "The King Family Show" 1965

STRAWBERRY SPINACH SALAD
(Laurette Walton)

Serves 12-15
10 oz. fresh spinach leaves
1 cup cut celery
1 pint strawberries, halved or quartered
¾ cup pecans
⅓ cup sugar

Sugared Pecans:
In small frying pan put pecan halves or pieces. Add 1/3 cup sugar and stir continuously over medium heat until sugar melts and coats nuts. Remove from heat and pour into a dish or aluminum foil. Make dressing and then combine all ingredients in large salad bowl.

Dressing:
½ cup sugar
4 green onions. sliced
2 tsp. salt
2 cups oil
2 tsp. dry mustard
3 Tbsp. poppy seeds
⅔ cup vinegar

Dressing:
Combine 1st 4 ingredients in blender. Slowly add oil and the rest of the ingredients. This makes a lot of dressing; you could cut in half.

THE ONLY TRUE BLUE CHEESE DRESSING
(Ric de Azevedo)

This is the greatest blue cheese dressing. Just ask my little brother, Cam, who, ever since he was little, has requested it whenever he eats at our home.

Serves 6
¼ cup red wine vinegar
⅓ cup salad oil
1 small container or bag of crumbled blue cheese
Coarse black pepper to taste
(Maybe.....just maybe, a pinch of Lawry's or salt)
Variation: Add 1 Tbsp. sour cream

Mix crumpled blue cheese into a small bowl with a fork adding red wine vinegar and salad oil. Add coarse black pepper. Don't over mix. I like it best over cold iceberg lettuce with large quartered tomatoes (with lots of coarse ground black pepper). Another variation: cut a head of iceberg lettuce into 4 large wedges and serve each person 1 wedge with or without quartered tomatoes, covered in dressing.

The Clarkes: Bob Clarke, Alyce King Clarke, Ric de Azevedo, Lex de Azevedo & Cam Clarke

SANTA ROSA VALLEY SALAD
(Jamie Miller)

Serves 12-15
3 chicken breasts (cooked and cubed)
1 box long grain and wild rice (cooked w/ seasoning from pkg.)
2 medium avocados
3 oz. peapods (Chinese/snow)
1 cup pecans, chopped
Juice from 1 lemon
4 green onions sliced
1 red pepper chopped
⅓ cup sugar

Dressing:
2 cloves garlic
1 Tbsp. Dijon mustard
½ tsp. sugar
¼ tsp. pepper
⅓ cup seasoned rice vinegar
½ tsp. salt
¼ cup oil

Make dressing in blender and refrigerate. Place pecans in small frying pan. Add 1/3 cup sugar and stir continuously over medium heat until sugar melts and coats nuts. Remove from heat and pour into a dish or tin foil. Mix all ingredients except avocado and pecans. Combine with dressing and refrigerate 2-4 hours. Add avocado and pecans before serving. Line bowl or platter with lettuce leaves for nice presentation.

KING FAMILY MANDARIN ORANGE SALAD
(King Sisters & King Cousins)

Every dang female in this family has claimed ownership of this recipe! One night on our summer tour, our performance ended shortly before we needed to leave for our scheduled flight. With no time to change out of our finale costumes, we all boarded the plane dressed in jeweled gowns and tuxedos. When it was time for the flight attendants to serve dinner (back in the days when meals were served), the boy cousins persuaded the crew to allow them to take over. With white towels draped over their arms and dressed in their formal tuxedos, the boys walked down the aisles, taking orders and serving the passengers in fine-dining fashion. The crew got into the spirit of it, watching as everyone in the coach section enjoyed first-class treatment!

Serves 8

1 can mandarin oranges, chilled and drained
½ cup sliced almonds
¼ - ½ cup sugar
1 cup celery, sliced
2 green onions, sliced
1 med. red onion sliced in thin rings
1- 2 avocados, sliced
1 head each Iceberg and Bibb lettuce, washed, chilled

Caramelize almonds with sugar by stirring over medium heat in pan until sugar is melted. Cool on buttered foil. Tear the lettuce and crunch the almonds. Add remaining ingredients into a large bowl and toss with dressing just before serving.

Luise's Dressing:
3 Tbsp. oil
1 Tbsp. vinegar
Lawry's
Pepper
Garlic Powder
Onion Powder

Vonnie's Dressing:
⅓ cup oil
⅓ cup rice vinegar
Lawry's
1 tsp. honey

Tina's Dressing:
¼ cup red wine vinegar
½ cup light olive oil
2 Tbsp. sugar
2 drops Tabasco sauce
¼ tsp. lemon pepper
1 Tbsp. chopped parsley
½ tsp. salt

Carolyn's Dressing:
¼ cup oil
2 Tbsp. sugar
2 Tbsp. malt vinegar
¼ tsp. salt
⅛ tsp. almond extract

CREAMY CUCUMBER AND TOMATO SALAD
(Xan Albright)

Serves 8
2 cucumbers, peeled and chopped
3 large tomatoes, chopped
1 red onion, chopped
Cilantro, chopped

Dressing:
1 small sour cream
Tabasco sauce, 4-5 drops
4-5 Tbsp. lemon juice
Salt and pepper to taste

Mix all together and chill. Delicious! Has a little bit of a bite.

RASPBERRY/VEGGIE SALAD MOLD
(Carolyn Cameron)

Served at our Driggs Family Reunion in Phoenix, Arizona, 1966. This recipe sounds odd but is delicious.

Serves 10

1 large pkg. raspberry Jell-O
¼ cup chives, chopped
2 celery stalks, chopped
1 green pepper, chopped
1 large can crushed pineapple (drained and set aside)
1 large can shredded beets (drained)
1 large container sour cream

Make Jell-O according to pkg. directions using juice from the crushed pineapple as part of the cold liquid. Place in a 2-quart Pyrex and add pineapple and beets. Let set until firm. Mix chives, celery and green pepper with sour cream and spread on top of firm Jell-O. Return to refrigerator until sour cream mixture is set and cold. Cut and serve.

King Cousins Tina, Carolyn, Xan & Ric in the kitchen at Lake Arrowhead, CA in 1998

RICE AND SHRIMP SALAD
(Jamie Miller)

Serves 6-8

1 MJB Herb & Butter Rice (cook according to package & cool)
½ lb. small shrimp
2 green onions, chopped
4 stalks celery, chopped
2 cans mandarin oranges

Dressing:
3 tbsp. chili sauce
¾ cup mayonnaise
½ tsp. Worcestershire

Mix all ingredients and chill. Whisk the dressing and put in fridge to "season." Serve on a lettuce leaf or inside a quartered tomato.

ASPARAGUS POTATO SALAD
(Wendy Lloyd)

Serves 6-8

5 russet or red potatoes, diced
½ lb. of thin asparagus

Dressing:
Juice from 1-2 lemons
¼ cup olive oil
Salt and allspice to taste

Bring diced potatoes to boil and simmer until soft but not mushy. Drain water and cool. Cut asparagus into 1" pieces. Very lightly steam asparagus and then cool. Put in serving bowl, sprinkle on dressing ingredients, toss and serve immediately for freshness.

CHICKEN PASTA PRIMAVERY SUPREME
(Phyllis Heim)

Serves 8-10

8 oz. bow tie pasta or your choice
1 Tbsp. Shilling Salad Supreme (or just Lawry's)
3 chicken breasts, cooked and cut into long slivers
Chicken can be mixed with a little pesto sauce after cutting
¼ cup pesto sauce (store bought – optional)
2 zucchinis
1 ea: red pepper, green pepper
1 small bunch broccoli cut into florets
½ bag baby carrots
1 box grape tomatoes
1 yellow squash
½ box frozen peas
1-2 cups Parmesan cheese
Bernstein's Cheese & Garlic salad dressing
(or other Italian dressing)

Cook pasta and cool. Sprinkle on Salad Supreme and salad dressing. Cover and refrigerate several hours or overnight. Taste! Adjust Salad Supreme and also use pepper (white pepper is awfully good). Vegetables should be cut in attractive ways, long slender if possible. Don't just make chunks out of them. Use any other vegetables that you like. Being careful not to cook them completely, blanch/boil carrots for 5 min, all other vegetables (except peas and tomatoes) for 2 min. Immediately after blanching, place these veggies in ice cold water to stop the cooking.

To serve: Combine blanched vegetables, chicken, tomatoes, frozen peas, more dressing to taste and Parmesan cheese (be generous). Taste! And adjust flavors. Serve in a bowl or on a platter with large lettuce leaves around the edges.

SUMMER SALAD

(Xan Albright)

A very different, delicious, and beautiful salad

Serves 10-12

1 head red leaf lettuce
1 large bag baby spinach
1 bunch asparagus
1 pint strawberries, halved
1 cantaloupe, chunked
1 pint cherry tomatoes, halved
8 oz. carton mushrooms, sliced
2 avocados, sliced or chunked
6 thin slices of any cheese
6 thin slices of deli ham

1-2 cups chicken or turkey chunks (if you want to make this a main dish)

Poppy Seed Dressing:
1 cup oil
½ cup tarragon vinegar
1 tsp. dry mustard
1 tsp. salt
½ cup sugar
1 Tbsp. poppy seeds
½ tsp. onion salt or 2 sliced green onions

Stir or shake in a jar until sugar is dissolved and dressing is thoroughly mixed. Let the dressing chill for 4-5 hours. Layer slices of cheese on slices of ham and tightly roll up into 6 small rolls. Put in a Ziploc. Chill these for several hours and then slice the cheese/ham into ½ inch pinwheels. Put back in fridge until ready to serve. Tear lettuce and spinach. Cut asparagus into 1½ inch pieces. Microwave for 3 minutes with a little water and put immediately in ice water to cool. Drain. Put all ingredients (except pinwheels and avocados) in a large bowl. Just before serving, add avocados, pinwheels, and toss salad with poppy seed dressing. (Except for slicing the avocados, salad can be prepared the day before and refrigerated in Ziplocs.)

WENDY'S FRESH SALAD
(Wendy Lloyd)

Serves 8

1 head red leaf lettuce, spinach or your choice
 (not iceberg or romaine – too bland)
1-2 Persian cucumbers, sliced in rounds
 (Trader Joe's or Iranian markets have them)
1 red onion, thinly sliced
2-3 tomatoes on the vine
Handful of fresh herbs (use one or more kinds):
mint, coriander, basil, oregano, thyme

Optional:
1 avocado, diced
½ lb. thin asparagus, cut into 1 ½" pieces

Fresh Lemon Dressing:
Juice from 1-2 lemons
¼ cup olive oil
Salt to taste
Allspice to taste

Cut up all vegetables and herbs in a large bowl. Just before serving, sprinkle dressing ingredients on salad and serve immediately for freshness. Delicious served with lamb sirloin steaks sprinkled with Lawry's Seasoned Salt and Lawry's Pepper. BBQ to your perfection (about 6 – 8 min on each side)

The King Sisters circa 1964 - Yvonne, Alyce, Marilyn & Luise.

Brunches & Vegetables

The King Cousins perform on the 1968 TV special "Easter with the King Family"

KING SISTERS '50s LUNCHEON SANDWICH LOAF
(Tina Cole)

This is a beautiful presentation for a special shower or party. Watch your company's surprised expressions when they discover this is a sandwich and not a cake, as it appears to be. Very hearty dish.

Serves 10-12
3-4 loaves unsliced white bread ordered from a bakery, dyed in pastel colors like pink, blue, green and yellow. Have the bakery slice each loaf horizontally (lengthwise) in at least 4-6 long slices.
2-3 (8 oz) bars of cream cheese for frosting
Filling #1 – tuna salad with mayo, chopped onion and celery
Filling #2 – pimiento cream cheese mixed with chopped walnuts
Filling #3 – deviled egg salad with mayo and chopped olives

Alternate colored slices of bread to build a 4-layer, 3 filling "sandwich cake". Place bottom slice on foiled tray. Spread filling #1, then 2nd slice of bread. Then filing #2 and 3rd slice, etc until topping with the 4th slice. Whip the cream cheese, adding a little milk in needed, until it's like a thick smooth frosting. Ice the entire loaf like a cake. You can add food coloring to some of the cream cheese for decorating if desired. To serve, slice it like a slice of cake and eat with a fork.

SPICED APPLES

(Yvonne King Burch)

Vonnie serves these spiced apples along with her Scrambled Eggs and Christmas "Snausages" every Christmas morning. These are also great for a brunch or even a dessert.

Serves 8

8 Rome apples
1 tsp. sherry wine or cooking sherry
1 Tbsp. white sugar
½ tsp. orange zest
1 Tbsp. brown sugar
8 Tbsp. butter (1 Tbsp. ea. apple)
1 tsp. cinnamon
Red food coloring
Orange juice
1 Tbsp. Red Hots candies
1 pint heavy cream, whipped & sweetened

For each apple:
Peel ½ way down. Core center but not all the way to the bottom. Mix white and brown sugars, cinnamon with enough orange juice to blend the dry ingredients. Pat this into the cored center. Add Red Hots, sherry, orange zest, and a dob of butter. Place upright in a large Pyrex dish filled with 1 inch of water. Pour red food color over the white of the peeled apple on top. Baste frequently making a red sauce throughout. Make a day ahead and chill in frig. Serve cold with whipped cream.

VONNIE'S GOURMET CHRISTMAS "SNAUSAGES"
(Yvonne King Burch)

Vonnie's stepson, Jeff, would devour these before they even reached the table. After he died from complications of 2 tours in Viet Nam, to this day, a plate of 4 "Snausages" is put on the Christmas breakfast table in honor of Jeff.

Makes 12 sausages

1 pkg. 12 "Jones Little Sausages" (or other brand), pricked with fork
1 yellow onion - finely chopped
1 cup consommé soup (non-diluted)
1 cup sherry wine or cooking sherry
1 Tbsp. butter
2 Tbsp. soft butter
1 ½ Tbsp. flour
2 heaping Tbsp. tomato puree

In skillet, melt butter, then add onions and sausages and fry until browned. Stir in Consommé, wine and tomato puree. Cover and simmer 15 minutes. Remove from heat, then remove sausages and wrap them in foil to keep warm. Combine soft butter and flour to make a pasty roux. Return skillet to heat and stir in roux until sauce is a smooth and thick gravy. Return sausages to skillet and stir to cover with sauce, adding more Consommé if too thick. Can be made a day ahead and reheated in oven or microwave.

VONNIE'S SCRAMBLED EGGS

(Yvonne King Burch)

Serves 10-12

1 dozen eggs
2 Tbsp. butter
¼ cup Half & Half
8 oz. cream cheese broken into chunks
Salt and pepper to taste

Beat eggs with Half & Half. Add salt and pepper. Melt butter in pan and pour in the egg mixture. Add chunks of cream cheese and blend in. This method will keep the eggs fluffy!

CHILI EGG PUFF

(Laurette Walton, Candy Brand, Anna de Azevedo)
Served at many brunch "showers" with fresh fruit, asparagus, and sweet rolls.

Serves 9

1 (7oz.) can chopped green chilies
1 large can evaporated milk
2 well beaten eggs
2 Tbsp. flour
Salt and pepper to taste
½ lb. each of Monterey Jack and cheddar cheese, grated

Place chilies in the bottom of a buttered 2 qt. Pyrex. Blend everything else and pour over chilies. Bake 350° for 30 minutes till golden. Can be served with salsa.

PUMPKIN PANCAKES
(Xan Albright)

Makes 5 dozen small 2" pancakes

½ cup solid packed pumpkin
2 eggs
1 cup milk
2 Tbsp. sugar
1 ¾ cup Bisquick
½ tsp. nutmeg
½ tsp. ginger
¼ cup salad oil
½ tsp. cinnamon

Beat eggs in a small bowl on high speed for 5 minutes, or until thick and lemon colored. Add oil and pumpkin. Mix. Sift and stir in remaining ingredients. Pour batter onto hot, ungreased griddle. Serve with hot Apple Cider Syrup.

Apple Cider Syrup:
1 cup sugar
2 Tbsp. cornstarch
½ tsp. pumpkin pie spice
2 cups apple cider or juice
2 Tbsp. lemon juice
¼ cup butter

Mix sugar, cornstarch, and spice in saucepan. Stir in cider and lemon juice. Cook, stirring, until thickens and boils for 1 min. Remove from heat and blend in butter.

Xan & cousin Ray on "The King Family Show"

TINA'S GERMAN PANCAKES

(Tina Cole, Yvonne King Burch)

Great for a brunch, Easter, or any special occasion, especially our cousins' reunions.

Serves 9

For 9x11 pan	For 8x8 pan
¼ cup butter	2 Tbsp. butter
1 ½ cups milk	1 cup milk
1 ½ cup flour	1 cup flour
1 tsp. salt	1 tsp. salt
9 eggs	6 eggs

Put butter in 9x11 Pyrex dish in 425° oven to melt (but not brown!) the butter. Meanwhile, place remaining ingredients in a blender on high for 30 seconds. Open over door and pull out dish just far enough to pour mixture into center of melted butter. Immediately close oven door. Bake for 18 minutes. Serve immediately, like a soufflé. It's all fluffed up!

Serve with any condiments you desire:

syrup
fresh berries
peaches
jam
nuts
sour cream
chunky applesauce
whipped cream

OATMEAL PANCAKES
(Phyllis Heim)

Serves 4-6

2 cups "Old fashioned" Oatmeal – not instant
2 cups milk
Place in bowl, cover and leave out on counter overnight.

In the morning, add:

½ cup flour	1 tsp. baking soda
2 eggs	1 Tbsp. sugar
1 tsp. baking powder	½ tsp. cinnamon
3 Tbsp. melted butter	

When ready to cook, combine all ingredients and mix thoroughly – grill until golden brown. Batter will be very thick – add more milk to thin down if desired. Serve with sautéed apples and raisins and Canadian bacon.

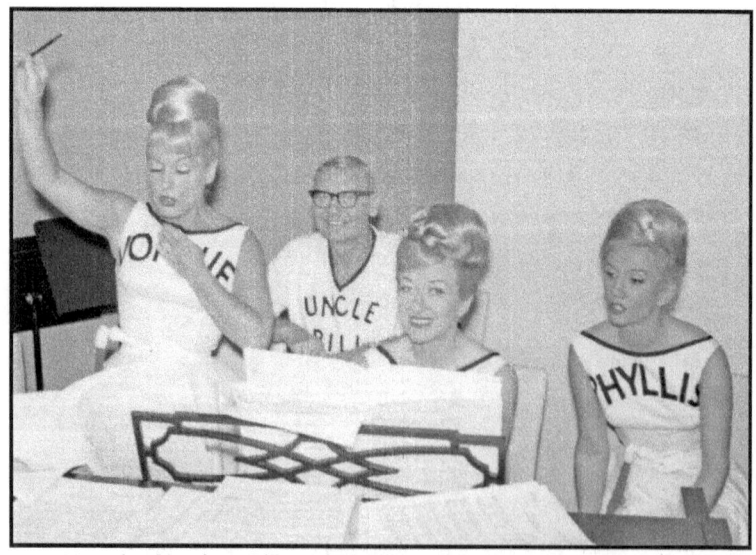

Vonnie, Maxine, Bill and Phyllis rehearsing for a live show

STUFFED FRENCH TOAST
(Noelle Sanderson)

Serves 6

8 oz. whipped cream cheese
1 pt. heavy cream, whipped & sweetened
4 eggs
⅔ cup milk
2 tsp. cinnamon
Sliced almonds, toasted
1 loaf Texas Toast
Maple syrup
1 jar orange marmalade

Beat together milk, eggs, and cinnamon. Dip bread into mixture and cook both sides in a flat plan, making the French toast. Lay one piece of toast on a plate; spread some marmalade and cream cheese on toast. Lay 2nd piece of toast on top. Dollop the "sandwich" with whipped cream and almonds. Add syrup.

AEBLESKIVERS
(Phyllis Heim)

Serves 8

1 pkg. dry yeast   ½ tsp. cardamom
¼ cup warm milk (for yeast)   2 cups flour
1 tsp. sugar   3 eggs
½ tsp. salt   2 cups milk

Dissolve dry yeast in ¼ cup warm milk in large bowl. Sift dry ingredients into a bowl, add eggs, milk. Mix well. Let rise about 2 hours. Bake in an Abelskiver pan. Serve hot with jam, powdered sugar, applesauce etc.

TUNA RITZ SANDWICHES
(Jamie Miller)

These are fabulous. They were served at Jamie's wedding and many an occasion. They can be made way ahead and frozen. Thaw for 1 hour.

Makes 40 sandwiches
1 loaf white sandwich bread
1 box Ritz crackers, crushed
8 oz. cream cheese, thinned with milk for an "icing" consistency
2 large cans of tuna

Make a good tuna salad – onion, Lawry's, celery seed, green onion, and mayo.

Cut white bread into small 2" circles with cutter or a drinking glass (3-4 each slice). Spread tuna on circle. Put bread on top. Frost entire sandwich (top, sides, and bottom) with cream cheese thinned with milk. Roll in crushed Ritz crackers.

Candy, Tina, Cathy, Carolyn & Jamie at a recording session for "The Kraft Summer Music Hall" 1966

TAHOE BRUNCH
(Carolyn Cameron)

In the 50's the King Sisters appeared every summer at Harrah's Club in Lake Tahoe, performing late into the night. After sleeping in, breakfast was often replaced by brunch. This is often served at family reunions.

Serves 12

1 ½ lbs. Italian sausage or 1 lb. crisp bacon, crumbled
½ cup butter
½ lb. mushrooms
2 thinly sliced yellow onions
1 tsp. ea. dry mustard & nutmeg
12 slices white bread, no crusts
¾ to 1 lb. cheddar cheese, grated
1 ½ cups milk
3 Tbsp. Dijon mustard
5 eggs
2 Tbsp. parsley
Salt & pepper to taste

In large skillet brown sausage and cut into bite size pieces. At same time melt ½ cup butter and sauté mushrooms and onions until tender. In a greased 11 X 17 shallow pan layer half the bread, mushroom mixture, sausage and cheese; repeat layers ending with cheese. In bowl, mix eggs, milk, both mustards and all other dry ingredients. Pour over sausage and cheese casserole. Cover and put in refrigerator overnight. When ready to cook, sprinkle with parsley and bake at 350° for 1 hour or until bubbly. Serve with fruit salad and crusty bread.

The King Sisters performing at Harrah's in 1956, joined by their kids

GLAZED CARROTS ÀLA DONNA
(Donna King Conkling)

Serves 6

1 bunch of carrots or bag of whole baby carrots
¼ cup butter
2 Tbsp. brown sugar

Boil sliced carrots or whole baby carrots. Toward the end, pour out water and sauté with butter and brown sugar until slightly browned. Add salt to taste.

SQUASH CASSEROLE
(Laurette Walton)

Serves 8

2 lb. yellow banana squash
1 grated carrot
1 grated onion
8 oz. sour cream
Cream of chicken soup
½ - 1 stick butter
1 small pkg. Pepperidge Farm Herb Stuffing.

Boil squash, strain and mash. Add carrot, onion and mix with the rest and ½ of the stuffing. Bake in 2-qt. pan and cover with rest of stuffing. Bake 350 ° for 1 hour until bubbly.

ZUCCHINI CASSEROLE
(Diana Driggs)

Serves 6

4 zucchini, cut in ¼" slices
½ cup onion, chopped
1 ½ cups herbed stuffing cubes
1 can cream of mushroom soup
1 cup Parmesan cheese

4 carrots, sliced
4 Tbsp. butter
½ cup water
8 oz. sour cream
chestnuts, sliced

In a saucepan sauté onion in butter until lightly browned. Add a bit of water and cook zucchini and carrots until tender. Drain any remaining water. Mix all ingredients together except cheese. Put into greased 8X8 pan. Sprinkle with cheese and bake at 350° for 15 min.

YUMMY CORN
(Donna King Conkling)

Serves 10

2 pkgs. frozen corn kernels
1 lb. bacon, crisp and crumbled
2 or 3 bunches chopped green onions

1 pt. sour cream
Lawry's to taste

Heat and cook corn in 1" water. Shortly before serving pour off liquid of cooked corn and add bacon, onions and toss. At last minute add Lawry's and sour cream. Serve immediately so that corn is still hot and sour cream doesn't curdle. You can reheat it a little if corn isn't hot enough. But be careful it doesn't curdle.

CREAMED CORN LIKE NO OTHER
(Carolyn Cameron)

Serves 8-10

2 (10 oz) pkgs frozen corn kernels, thawed
¼ cup Parmesan cheese, grated
2 Tbsp. butter
1 cup whole milk
2 Tbsp. flour
¼ tsp. ground pepper
1 cup heavy cream
1 tsp. salt
2 Tbsp. sugar

In a skillet over medium heat, combine the corn, cream, salt, sugar, pepper and butter. Whisk together the milk and flour, and stir into the corn mixtures. Cook stirring over medium heat until the mixture is thickened, and corn is cooked through. Remove from heat, and stir in the Parmesan cheese until melted. Serve hot.

FRESH GREEN BEANS
(Grandma Pearl Driggs)

Grandma Pearl would cook these on the stovetop for hours. Now we all know to cook vegetables for a much shorter time in order to retain the vitamin potency, so the "time's are a-changing."

1 lb. fresh green beans
3 strips uncooked bacon
Pepper to taste
Ham hock
2 Tbsp. Lawry's

Cut the ends off the green beans and remove the strings. In a covered medium kettle, bring everything to a boil and simmer for 30min-1 hour. Remove the ham hock before serving.

PICNIC BAKED BEANS
(Carolyn Cameron, Xan Albright)

The King Family would find any excuse to have a picnic: Memorial Day, Veteran's Day, even Groundhog Day if it fell on a Saturday! We'd choose a park, bring kites if it was windy, Frisbees, baseball equipment, a football. Because there were so many of us (usually about 50-60 would come out to a picnic) it was a perfect set-up for relay races. We'd line up for a sack race, 3-legged race, pull your team through the hula-hoop race, squeeze the sponge full of water into a bucket race, egg-in-spoon race...you name it, we played it! Of course, each team included kids of all ages—and some older folks too! Then we'd end up playing a rousing game of Charades, with the movie, song, and book titles created by the opposing team. It was intense competition but lots of laughs too... no one can forget Uncle Alvino trying to act out the song "Vaya Con Dios"!

Serves 10

1 large can pork 'n beans	1 large onion, chopped
1 can kidney beans	½ cup molasses
1 can pinto beans	½ cup brown sugar
1 (28 oz) can diced tomatoes	1-2 Tbsp. mustard
½ c. brown sugar	

Drain all beans and tomatoes well. Put in crockpot. Add all other ingredients and cook on low for several hours.

CARROT SOUFFLÉ
(Tina Cole)

Different, delicious, and never fails! Even those who can't abide carrots will ask for the recipe!

Serves 8

2 cups carrots, cooked and pureed*
2 Tbsp. onions, minced or grated
2 tsp. lemon juice
½ cup butter, softened
¼ cup sugar
1 Tbsp. flour
1 tsp. salt
¼ tsp cinnamon
1 cup milk
3 eggs

*Carrots may be cooked and pureed hours ahead of time, adding the lemon juice and covering tightly until ready to mix. Beat all ingredients together until smooth. Pour into a 2-quart, lightly buttered soufflé dish or casserole. Bake, uncovered, in a preheated 350° oven for 45 min. - 1 hour until the center is firm to the touch.

**Publicity photo of The Four King Cousins
(Candy, Carolyn, Tina & Cathy), circa 1968**

CREAMED POTATOES AND PEAS
(Grandma Pearl Driggs)

Serves 6-8
4-6 potatoes peeled:
(Grandma's favorite variety was "new potatoes")
1 cup of fresh or frozen peas

White sauce:
6 Tbsp. butter
6 Tbsp. flour
3 cups milk

Boil the potatoes until soft but not mushy. Cut them into small pieces. Make a white sauce by melting butter over low heat and blending in flour. Add milk and cook quickly, stirring constantly till mixture comes to a boil, thickens, and is smooth. Just before serving, put potatoes and peas in the sauce. Cook for 1 or 2 minutes to protect the peas.

Grandma Pearl Driggs on "The King Family Show" 1965

POTATOES O'BRIEN
(Shauna Elliott)

Serves 8-10

1 large bag O'Brien potatoes (frozen)
1 ½ cups Cornflakes, crushed into ¼ cup melted butter
½ cup chopped onions
3 Tbsp. butter
3 oz. cream cheese
½ cup cheddar cheese (or more)

Sauté onions in butter. Mix into the rest of ingredients. Top with cornflakes. Put in 9X13 dish and bake at 400° for 45 minutes.

POTATOES OLIVER
(Tina Cole)

Number of servings: you decide

Russet potatoes (1 per/person) (can use red potatoes, too)
½ cup butter - melted
1 bunch Scallions, finely chopped
Kosher Salt

Slice potatoes into thin circles (like potato chips). Depending on the amount of potatoes, use 8X8 or 9X13 Pyrex. Keep slices together in potato shape and lay each whole, sliced potato end to end in a Pyrex, so that you have rows of slices all together. Push the potatoes so they splay out a little (like dominoes). Pour butter over potatoes. Sprinkle with onions. Bake at 425° for 1 hour uncovered, basting every 20 minutes. Sprinkle Kosher Salt very liberally over tops of potatoes and continue cooking and basting another 30 minutes.

CANDIED SWEET POTATOES & APPLES
(Jennifer Suttner)

Delicious, I promise!

Serves 8

2 lb. sweet potatoes, peeled
3 large apples, cored and cut into ½" rings
1 cup firmly packed light brown sugar
½ cup apple cider
1 cup butter
¼ tsp. salt
1 tsp. vanilla

Cut sweet potatoes in half. Cook in boiling water 10 minutes. Drain and cut into ½ "slices. Combine brown sugar, butter, cider and salt in a saucepan. Boil 10 minutes. Remove from heat and stir in vanilla. Layer sweet potatoes and apples in a greased 9x13. Pour glaze over slices. Bake uncovered at 400° for 1 hour basting with glaze after 30 minutes. Delicious, I promise!

The King Sisters performing on "The Chevy Show" in 1959

BAKED FRUIT

(Alyce King Clarke)

Serves 6

1 large can half peaches (reserve the syrup)
2 bananas sliced lengthwise and quartered
2 Tbsp. brown sugar
1 can Bing cherries
1 cup raisins
Nutmeg

Arrange peaches, bananas, and cherries in 8X8 Pyrex dish. Pour peach syrup over. Add raisins. Sprinkle over brown sugar and nutmeg. Bake 325° for 20 minutes.

King Sister Alyce and her elegant table setting for Christmas

SPACK MORTENSEN'S DILL PICKLES
(Chick Rey)

Spack Mortensen is the wife of Art Mortensen. Art was a cousin of Luise and her siblings and a flyer who ran the Ogden Utah Airport for years and took the Rey family on fishing/pack trips in Idaho, Wyoming, etc. and was a great pal of Alvino's.

25 (4") pickling cucumbers
The following depends on the amount of jars being used:
Fresh cloves of garlic, peeled
Fresh dill sprigs
Dried red chili peppers
Mason jars (quarts) with seals and lids
1 cup granulated pickling salt
3 quarts water
1 quart cider vinegar

Wash cukes and pack in hot, clean quart bottles. Add to EACH quart of pickles: 1 clove of garlic, 2 sprigs of fresh dill and 1 red pepper. Make a brine by combining the pickling salt, water and cider vinegar. Bring this mixture to a boil in a large kettle, and fill jars of pickles to within ½ inch of top with hot brine. Have mason jar lids and rings sterilizing in pan of boiling water. Place each jar of pickles with hot brine in microwave for one minute on high, one at a time. Remove, wipe off sealing edge of jar, put jar lid on and tighten ring. Turn jar upside down on towel on counter. Repeat until all quarts of pickles have been "processed" in microwave. When they are all completely cooled (a few hours or overnight), turn upright and check to be sure that each one has sealed. These are the crispest, most wonderful dill pickles you'll ever eat. If one does not seal for some reason, just keep it in the fridge for a week or so to cure and enjoy.

Desserts

The King Kids Laurette, Adam, Jonathan, Debbie, Steve, Cam & Susannah enjoying snowballs during a break between concerts

DONNA'S CHOCOLATE HOT FUDGE SAUCE
(Donna King Conkling)

Served at practically every family party from the '60's-'80's. A traditional family favorite!

Serves 8-10

1 ½ cups baking cocoa
3 cups sugar
1 ½ cups milk
3 Tbsp. Karo Syrup
2-3 Tbsp. butter
1 Tbsp. vanilla
¼ tsp. salt

Cook unsweetened cocoa powder, sugar, milk and Syrup in a small kettle over medium heat stirring constantly until they are dissolved and syrup begins to gently boil. Take off stove and add butter, vanilla, and salt.

CHOCOLATE FONDUE
(Cathy Green)

Simple and quick

Serves 4

½ cup heavy cream
8 oz. semi sweet chocolate chips, melted in microwave
1 tsp. vanilla

Heat cream gently in kettle until it's bubbling around edges. Do not scald. Add melted chips and vanilla and mix on low heat until smooth and thickened. Serve with strawberries, bananas, or any fruit of your choice.

TINA'S SINFULLY DELICIOUS "FAGAGA" HOT FUDGE
(Tina Cole)

Served at practically every family party from the '90's till now! A newer family favorite! "Fagaga" is the King Family's title for any of Tina's ridiculously rich and incredibly delicious recipes.

Serves 8

2 ½ squares Baker's unsweetened chocolate
1 cup heavy cream or Half & Half
¾ cup powdered sugar
4 Tbsp. butter
1 level tsp. salt
1 tsp. vanilla

Melt butter and chocolate and salt in saucepan over medium heat - stirring constantly. Remove from heat. When melted add powdered sugar (all at once) and stir until completely blended into a ball. Return to heat and slowly pour in cream - a little at a time - stirring constantly (using only as much as needed) to reach desired thickness. Bring to low boil stirring constantly until thick, smooth, and glossy.

Phyllis, Tina & friend backstage after a King Family concert

"PIONEER" APPLESAUCE DESSERT
(Donna King Conkling)

This was a simple and affordable dessert Grandma Pearl would serve her 8 children; especially refreshing on a warm summer night

Serves 6

12 large Graham Crackers, crushed
1 large jar of applesauce
1 pint heavy cream, whipped and sweetened

In a parfait glass spoon 2 Tbsp. crushed graham crackers. Add several spoonfuls of applesauce and top off with a dollop of whipped cream. Then repeat another layer until you reach the top of the glass.

**Grandma Pearl Driggs with her eight children:
Karleton, Maxine, Marilyn, Bill, Luise, Vonnie, Alyce & Donna**

PUMPKIN SURPRISE

(Tina Cole, Jamie Miller, Candy Brand)

A wonderful Fall presentation. Serve on a platter with autumn leaves around it.

Serves 10-12

1 medium pumpkin (taller than wide with a good stem)
10 green apples (Granny Smith or Pippin), peeled & cut into bite-size chunks
1 cup pecans or walnuts, chopped
½ cup solid packed pumpkin
1 cup sugar
½ cup brown sugar
1 Tbsp. cinnamon
1 tsp. nutmeg
Juice of 1 lemon, 1 orange
1 tsp. cloves
1 cup raisins

Cut the lid of pumpkin so it will not be able to fall inside. Then hollow out and clean as if for a jack-o-lantern. Cut face, but not completely through the meat - only through the top layer of skin so there are no holes. Mix together rest of ingredients in a large bowl, then spoon into the prepared pumpkin. Replace lid. Spray a sturdy cookie sheet with vegetable spray and place pumpkin on it. Bake at 350° for 1-1½ hours depending on the thickness of the sides of the pumpkin. Apples should be crisp-tender and the skin of the pumpkin nice and dark. Ladle mixture right from the pumpkin over vanilla ice cream. (If pressed for time, the ingredients can be baked in a 9x13 Pyrex without using a carved pumpkin and bake for 30-45 min.)

TRIFLE CHRISTMAS PUDDING
(Donna King Conkling)

Donna made this every year for the whole family at Christmastime. It's beautiful and festive!

Serves 10

1 angel food cake or pound cake torn into bite-sized pieces
2 large boxes vanilla pudding, prepared as directed on box (instant or regular), and chilled
1 large jar raspberry jam
1 large jar apricot or peach jam
1 or more pints of heavy cream, whipped and lightly sugared

This is a layered dessert, so put in a large or tall pretty glass bowl. Start with pieces of angel food cake. Cover with pudding. Then cover with thin layers of both jams, finally with whipped cream. Repeat layers as high as you want, but end with whipped cream. Garnish with fresh berries at the top. Be sure you can see the colors of the jam from the outside. Increase amounts of ingredients depending on your group.

Donna & Alyce checking place cards

AUNT LILLY'S MAYONNAISE CAKE
(Lilly McBurney)

Each King Sister living or dead claims this as her own. But if the truth be known, according to Donna Conkling, the recipe belongs to Lilly, Alvino Rey's mother. Aunt Hazel won 1st place in a baking contest with this recipe. Don't let the title scare you off... this is a delicious chocolate cake!

The King Family members are big fans of the 4th of July. Our celebrations last the entire day and into the evening. It's a day of swimming, red, white and blue attire, all-day appetizers, games, dinner, homemade ice cream, and finally culminating in an evening program devoted to the spirit of the holiday.

One particular year our program went something like this: It began with a parade of all the young children, adorned in their patriotic wear. Then there were a series of historical vignettes, which included all the children and teenagers. Dressed in costumes suggesting George Washington, Thomas Jefferson, Patrick Henry, and Paul Revere, a child or teen stood and shouted out a few of that character's most famous quotations. Another costumed group, standing smashed together in a refrigerator box, acted out Washington's "Crossing the Delaware." Then suddenly a group of little cousins, carrying cardboard boxes labeled "coffee," "tea," or "sugar" made a dash for the swimming pool where they tossed in their boxes, enacting the Boston Tea Party.

Next, an uncle stood and related what eventually happened to the signers of the Declaration of Independence. Someone sang a solo. Teens made short comments about what it was like to be a young American today. Finally a 6-year old dressed in her mother's white nightgown, holding a book in one hand and "sparklers" in the other, was wheeled in on a dolly – a very poised and solemn Statue of Liberty. When she stepped off the dolly onto her platform, taking her part very seriously, the rest of us tried not to laugh. But then a little voice began – one child's voice singing "God Bless America." Soon other voices joined in, and within seconds all of us were singing the inspiring song in full harmony. Someone counted 102 of us that day and there wasn't a dry eye anywhere in the group.

Our mothers were right when they taught us that you had to go to a little trouble to make a memory. That day was proof of it—the food, the decorations, the fun, and the celebration of all things American will never be forgotten by any of us.

Part I:
Sift together:
1 cup sugar   1 ½ cups flour
1 tsp. cinnamon   ½ cup unsweetened cocoa
½ tsp. (each) nutmeg, ground cloves, allspice, and salt

Part II:
1 cup boiling water   1 cup dates, pitted and chopped
1 tsp. baking soda   1 cup chopped walnuts

Put hot water with soda in pan with dates and nuts. Cover. Let stand while preparing next part.

Part III:
1 egg
1 cup oil

Beat egg adding a little oil at a time, beating constantly until it makes a mayonnaise. Mix all of the cake ingredients together. Bake in 2 greased, floured cake pans. Bake 350° for 30 to 35 minutes.

Icing:

Donna's Icing	Liza Rey's Icing
6 Tbsp. butter	4 Tbsp. butter
2 sqs unsweetened chocolate	8 sqs unsweetened chocolate
2 cups powdered sugar	¾ cup powdered sugar
¼ tsp. salt	¾ cup sugar
3 egg whites beaten stiff	¼ tsp. salt
	3 egg whites

Melt butter and chocolate. Mix in ½ of the total powdered sugar. Mix in salt and egg whites. Add remaining powdered sugar, putting it in only 2 Tbsp. at a time. Beat vigorously.

"COMPANY" CAKE
(Donna King Conkling)

Serves 8-10 as it is a 3-layer cake
1 ready-made Angel Food cake
½ gallon your choice of ice cream (Donna prefers mocha flavor), softened
1 pint heavy cream, whipped and lightly sweetened
6 oz. semi sweet chocolate chips, melted

Slice cake into three layers. Ice thickly the top of each layer with mocha ice cream (if you don't want the mocha flavor, you can use chocolate ice cream or any flavor of your choice.) Stack the 3 layers of cake & ice cream. Freeze the cake with ice cream in freezer. When cake is completely frozen, whip the cream and very lightly sweeten it. Ice the entire cake with whipped cream and freeze again. Then melt approximately 6 oz. chocolate chips and drip it over the top and down the sides of the frozen cake. Store in freezer.

BANANA CAKE WITH QUICK CARAMEL FROSTING
(Jamie Miller, Sarah Thomas)

Serves 8 –10 as it is a tall cake

2 medium-sized ripe bananas, peeled & mashed (about 1 cup)
1 pkg. plain yellow cake mix
½ cup light brown sugar
1 Tbsp. cinnamon
1 cup water
½ cup vegetable oil
3 eggs

Grease and flour 2 (9-inch) round cake pans. Combine cake mix, sugar and cinnamon. Add the mashed bananas, water, oil, and eggs. Blend on low 1 minute and then medium for 2 minutes more. Bake 350° for 30-33 minutes until cakes are light brown. Cool 10 minutes and remove from pans.

Filling:
½ pint heavy cream, whipped and sweetened with sugar
1 ripe banana, sliced, mixed with 1 Tbsp. lemon juice
¼ cup Cool Whip

Beat cream and sweeten to taste. Add in Cool Whip (helps keep whip cream from separating). Spread on cooled cake round (you may not need all the filling but try to make a thick layer). Cover the layer with sliced bananas. Put other round cake layer on top. Refrigerate.

Frosting:
½ cup <u>light</u> brown sugar, packed
½ cup <u>dark</u> brown sugar, packed
2 cups powdered sugar, sifted
½ cup chopped pecans or walnut

¼ cup milk
½ cup butter
1 Tbsp. vanilla

Place the butter and brown sugars in heavy saucepan over medium heat. Stir until mixture boils; cook about 2 min. Continue to stir and add the milk. Bring back to a boil, then remove from heat. Add powdered sugar and vanilla. Beat with a wooden spoon until smooth. Use immediately while still warm, or thin with hot water as you frost. Sprinkle immediately with nuts. Keep refrigerated.

CHOCOLATE OR STRAWBERRY ANGEL FOOD CAKE
(Xan Albright)

1 ready-made Angel Food cake
Choose 1 of the flavors below to fill and top the cake:

Chocolate flavor
Mix together:
1 pint heavy cream, whipped
1 ½ cup powdered sugar
¾ cup cocoa (unsweetened)
¼ tsp. salt

Strawberry flavor
Mix together:
1 pint heavy cream, whipped
1 carton of strawberries, crushed

Cut off top of angel food cake. Make a tunnel about 2 inches deep in bottom portion of cake. Don't cut all the way through to the bottom. Fill the tunnel with either the chocolate or strawberry-flavored whipped cream. Replace the cut off, top portion of cake and ice the entire cake with the remainder of the cream. Make chocolate swirls on top and cover with blanched almonds.

"DEVILISH" CHOCOLATE CAKE
(Xan Albright, Jamie Miller)
Fabulously rich - serve a small slice with a scoop of ice cream!

1 pkg. Devil's food cake or dark chocolate fudge cake mix
1 small pkg. chocolate instant pudding mix
4 eggs
1 cup sour cream
½ cup warm water
½ cup vegetable oil
1 ⅓ cups semisweet chocolate chips
Powdered sugar to sprinkle (optional)

Spray Bundt pan with oil and dust with flour. Place the cake mix, pudding mix, eggs, sour cream, warm water, and oil in a large mixing bowl. Blend with a mixer on low speed for 1 minute and then 2 - 3 minutes on medium speed. Fold in the chocolate chips and pour batter into pan. Cook at 350° for 45-50 minutes and cool completely. Turn out onto a plate and dust with powdered sugar (optional).

A real King Family Thanksgiving dinner!

GINGERBREAD WITH WARM LEMON SAUCE
(Candy Brand)

Serves 10

2 ½ cups flour	½ cup oil
2 tsp. baking powder	½ cup sugar
½ tsp. baking soda	2 eggs
½ tsp. salt	1 cup molasses
⅛ tsp. ground cloves	1 cup boiling water
1 tsp. ginger	1 tsp. cinnamon

Sift flour, baking powder, soda, salt and all 3 spices. Cream oil, sugar and eggs; beat well. Add molasses and dry ingredients and blend. Add boiling water and mix well. Pour into a greased 9x13 pan. Bake at 350° for 45 minutes. Serve warm with lemon sauce and sweetened whipped cream.

Lemon Sauce:

½ cup sugar	2 Tbsp. lemon juice
1 Tbsp. cornstarch	Dash of salt
1 cup boiling water	2 Tbsp. butter
Dash of nutmeg	Grated lemon zest from 1 lemon

Mix sugar and cornstarch in saucepan. Gradually stir in water. Cook over medium heat, stirring constantly until mixture thickens and boils. Boil and stir one minute, remove from heat. Stir in remaining ingredients and serve warm.

STRAWBERRY CAKE W/ STRAWBERRY CREAM CHEESE FROSTING
(Laurette Walton)

This has a very old fashioned, homemade taste to it, almost like a delicious carrot cake.

Cake:
1 pkg. plain white cake mix
1 small package strawberry Jell-o.
1 ½ cups fresh strawberries, then mashed with juice included
½ cup milk (whole, lowfat or nonfat – it doesn't seem to matter)
1 cup grated coconut (the cake is so sweet that unsweetened would be good if you could find it)
4 eggs
1 cup oil
½ cup chopped pecans

Grease 2 (9 inch) round cake pans. Blend everything except coconuts and nuts on low speed for 1 minute. At medium speed, blend 2 more minutes. Fold in coconut and pecans. Bake at 350° for 28-30 minutes (note: I have to bake at least 33-35 minutes or my center is raw so definitely test--also, when it is done, the top will be definitely light brown, and sides will pull away from pan.) Cool completely.

Frosting:
8 oz. package cream cheese, softened
½ cup butter, softened
3 ½ cups powdered sugar
¾ cup fresh strawberries, then mashed with juice included
½ cup grated coconut
½ cup chopped pecans

Combine cream cheese and butter and beat till smooth. Add sugar and strawberries. Blend on low speed until the sugar is thoroughly mixed in. Mix on medium for 1 minute. Fold in coconut and pecans. Frost the cake between layers, and top and sides.

RAW APPLE CAKE
(Xan, Erin, Annie Albright)
Wonderful holiday dessert

2 cups fresh apples, grated finely	1 cup flour
2 Tbsp. lemon juice	1 tsp. cinnamon
½ cup butter	1 tsp. soda
¾ cup sugar	¼ tsp. nutmeg
1 egg	1 tsp. vanilla
½ tsp. salt	½ cup chopped nuts (optional)

Peel and grate apples; sprinkle with lemon juice, then set aside. Cream butter and sugar and add in egg. Sift dry ingredients together and add to butter mixture. Add apples, vanilla, and nuts. Bake at 350° in 8 X 8 inch pan for 35 – 40 minutes (you can double the recipe for a 9 X13 – serves 12). Serve with Hot Apple Topping and whipped cream. So yummy for holiday time!

Hot Apple Topping:
3-4 chopped apples of your choice
½ -1 pkg. (3oz.) instant vanilla pudding
1 cup (or more) fruit juice (apple or apple/cranberry)
1 tsp. cinnamon
2-3 Tbsp. toasted almonds, chopped (optional)
Spices: sugar and nutmeg (if needed, to taste)
Sauté apples in pudding packet and fruit juice (makes a "thickening") until soft. Add the rest. Serve over apple cake, or ice cream, or waffles.

GREAT CARROT CAKE!
(Cathy Green)

Serves 12

Sift:

2 cups flour	1 tsp. baking powder
1 ½ tsp. baking soda	1 tsp. salt
1 tsp. cinnamon	2 cups sugar

Blend all ingredients below and then add sifted, dry ingredients to mixture.

1½ cups oil (can reduce oil to 1 cup and add 1 additional cup applesauce)
4 eggs, 1 at a time
2 cups carrots, grated and peeled
1 can crushed pineapple
1-1 ½ cups chopped walnuts, optional

Bake in 9x13 Pyrex for 35-45 minutes at 350°. Test in center w/ toothpick.

Cream cheese frosting:

¾ cube butter	8 oz. cream cheese
1 box powdered sugar	1 tsp. vanilla

Blend all together and frost.

"The King Family Show" 1965

CHOCOLATE VELVET CREAM CAKE
(Sarah Thomas)

1 box chocolate fudge cake mix

<u>Velvet cream</u>
⅔ cup cocoa powder
2 cups heavy cream
8 oz. cream cheese
¾ cup powdered sugar
2 tsp. vanilla

<u>Chocolate Ganache</u>
⅔ cup heavy cream
6 oz. semi sweet chocolate chips

Make one chocolate fudge cake mix according to box directions. Bake in two 8" or 9" cake pans. Cool completely and cut each layer in two (making 4 total layers).

Velvet cream:
Beat heavy cream with cream cheese. Add powdered sugar, cocoa, and vanilla. Mix.

Chocolate Ganache:
Cook heavy cream and choc chips until it bubbles, Chill.

Fill each cake layer with thick amounts of velvet cream. Keep the top layer plain. Pour whole batch of Ganache over the top and sides of cake. Keep dessert chilled.

PUMPKIN CAKE
(Tina Cole)

Serves 12

Part 1:

1 box of yellow cake mix - minus 1 cup
1 egg - beaten
½ cup melted butter

Part 2:

1 large can solid pack pumpkin
3 eggs - beaten
⅔ cup evaporated milk
½ cup brown sugar
½ cup granulated sugar
1 tsp. cinnamon
½ tsp. each - salt, ground cloves, ground ginger, nutmeg

Part 3:

1 cup yellow cake mix
2 Tbsp. brown sugar
1 cup pecan bits
2 Tbsp. granulated sugar
½ tsp. cinnamon
3 Tbsp. melted butter

Mix Part 1 items together and pat into the bottom of a Pam-sprayed 9x13 Pyrex.

Blend Part 2 items and pour over cake mixture already in the pan.

Stir together Part 3 items with a fork into a "crumble" and sprinkle on top of Part 2. Dot with cold butter. Bake at 400° for 15 minutes, then turn oven down to 325° and bake an additional 50 min. Cool and serve topped with sweetened whipped cream (tastes even better the next day).

SOUR CREAM POPPY SEED CAKE
(Diana Driggs)

1 box yellow cake mix
1 small pkg. vanilla instant pudding and pie filling
4 eggs
1 cup sour cream
½ cup oil
½ cup orange juice or water
¼ cup poppy seeds.

Beat cake mix, pudding mix, eggs, sour cream, oil and juice in large bowl on low speed just to moisten. Beat on medium speed 2 minutes. Stir in poppy seeds. Spoon into greased and floured 12 cup fluted tube pan or 10 inch tube pan. Bake at 350° for 50 to 55 minutes. Cool completely and remove from pan. Cool completely on wire rack. Sprinkle with powdered sugar, if desired.

A King Family bike ride in Toronto

LEMON-PLUM "TOUR" CAKE
(Tina Cole, Carolyn Cameron)

After traveling all day in our tour bus during a summer of performances, our concert host opened our bus door and walked on with platters filled with this delicious cake. It was all devoured to the last crumb. We begged for the recipe and have been making it ever since!

Cake:
2 cups self rising flour
2 cups sugar
1 tsp. cinnamon
1 tsp. ground cloves
3 eggs
1 cup oil
½ can of plums, drained
2 Tbsp. plum jam
2 (4 oz) jars of Earth's Best Organic baby food Apples & Plums (Stage 2)
1 tsp. tapioca buds (optional)
(Note: The previous 4 items are a substitute for 2 bottles of Jr. Baby Food Plums, which we can no longer find. If you can find them, your recipe is easier!)

Grease and flour a Bundt pan. Sift dry ingredients together and set aside. In mixer, beat eggs until light. Continue beating, and slowly pour oil in a thin stream into eggs to make a thin mayonnaise. In food processor or blender, puree the plums, plum jam, baby food, and optional tapioca. You will use only 1 cup + 3 Tbsp of this (Put unused portion in fridge to use as jam). Add plum mixture to egg/oil mixture. Then mix in the dry ingredients until just blended. Do not overbeat. Pour batter into Bundt pan and bake at 350° for 1 hour and 10 min. (toothpick comes out clean).

Glaze:
¼ cup butter, melted
Juice & zest of 1 large lemon
1 ½ cups powdered sugar

Mix butter, lemon juice and zest together and blend in powdered sugar. As soon as cake comes out of oven (leave cake in pan) pour ½ the glaze over the hot cake (this will become the bottom of the cake). When cool, turn cake onto serving plate and drizzle remaining glaze over top and sides of cake. Dust with powdered sugar if desired.

Another tour story: The family had just finished a show in Colorado and arrived at the airport about an hour before departure. Rushed and hungry, thirty-two of us burst into the one coffee shop in the terminal which was about to close at 11 pm. The one waitress began to take orders, looking fairly overwhelmed. Realizing she and the cook were outnumbered, one of the boy cousins jumped up and announced, "Let's help out!" Without hesitating, the girl cousins started taking orders while a couple of aunts and uncles went back to the kitchen to speed up the process. Thirty-two sandwiches, soups, and salads later, the cook and waitress were relieved and thrilled with the late-night tips in their pockets. The family boarded the plane happy and satisfied, laughing and chatting about a possible new venture into the restaurant business!

CROCKPOT CHOCOLATE CHIP PUDDING CAKE
(Cherilyn Church)

Serves 12

1 pkg. <u>plain</u> Devil's food cake mix (no pudding in the mix)
1 small pkg. chocolate instant pudding
16 oz. sour cream
4 large eggs
¾ cup vegetable oil
2 tsp. pure vanilla extract
1 cup water
6 oz. pkg. semisweet chocolate chips
Vegetable oil cooking spray (for misting the slow cooker)
Ice cream of your choice for serving....

Place the cake mix, pudding mix, sour cream, eggs, oil and vanilla in a large mixing bowl. Add 1 cup of water. Beat with an electric mixer on low speed until blended, 30 seconds. Then increase the mixer speed to medium and beat 2 minutes longer. Fold in the chocolate chips. Mist the bottom and side of a 4 ½ x 6 quart Crockpot with vegetable oil cooking spray. Transfer the batter to the Crockpot and cover it. Cook the cake until it is quite puffed in the center and begins to pull away from the side of the cooker, 3 ½ hours on high heat or 6 ½-7 hours on low heat. Spoon the warm cake into serving bowls. Serve with your favorite ice cream.

MISSISSIPPI MUD CAKE
(Tina Cole)

Makes 9 large or 12 small servings

1 cup butter, melted	2 Tbsp. vanilla
¾ cup unsweetened cocoa	1 ½ cups flour
2 cups sugar	½ tsp. salt
4 eggs	1 cup walnuts, chopped (optional)

Beat butter, cocoa, and sugar well. Add eggs one at a time beating well after each. Mix in vanilla. Combine the flour and salt and beat into batter. Stir in walnuts. Pour into greased and floured or sprayed 9x13 pan. Bake 25-30 minutes at 350°. Prepare frosting while cake is baking to use immediately after taking cake out of oven.

Frosting:

1 cup butter, melted	¼ cup cocoa
1 tsp. salt	1 tsp. vanilla
1 lb. box powdered sugar	⅓ cup milk
2 cups mini marshmallows	

Add butter, cocoa, salt, vanilla, powdered sugar, and milk. Beat well. While fresh out of oven, top hot cake with marshmallows, then pour frosting over top of marshmallows. Swirl with spatula as marshmallows melt.

CHOCOLATE PISTACHIO CAKE
(Xan Albright)

Cake:
½ cup pecans or walnuts, chopped
½ cup semisweet chocolate chips
1 small pkg. pistachio instant pudding mix
1 pkg. white cake mix
½ cup chocolate syrup
½ cup sugar
1 cup water
½ cup oil
4 eggs

Lightly spray a Bundt pan with oil and flour. Sprinkle the nuts and chocolate chips evenly in the bottom of the pan. Set aside. In a mixing bowl place cake mix, pudding mix, sugar, water, oil and eggs. Blend with mixer on low speed for 1 minute then 2 minutes on medium speed. Take out ¾ cup of the batter and mix it with chocolate syrup in a small bowl and set aside. Pour the remaining batter into the prepared pan. Pour the chocolate batter over the top, keeping the chocolate away from the pan edges. Swirl the chocolate batter into the white batter using a dinner knife. Bake 55-60 min. at 350°. Remove and cool completely, then turn out on a plate. Glaze the cooled cake with chocolate glaze.

Chocolate Glaze:
2 Tbsp. unsweetened cocoa powder
1 ¼ cups powdered sugar
¼ cup heavy cream
2 Tbsp. butter
1 tsp. vanilla

Melt the butter in a saucepan over low heat. Add the cocoa powder and cream and stir until the mixture thickens. Do not boil. Remove the pan from burner and stir in the powdered sugar and vanilla until the mixture is smooth. Spoon the glaze over the cooled cake.

SELF-FILLED CUPCAKES
(Jani Driggs)

Makes 20-24 cupcakes
1 chocolate cake mix, make according to directions on box
Filling:
8 oz cream cheese
⅓ cup sugar
Dash of salt
1 egg
6 oz chocolate chips

Prepare the cake mix by following directions on box but don't bake yet. Fill muffin tins ¾ full with batter. Cream together the filling mixture, stirring in the chocolate chips. Drop a spoonful of the cream cheese mixture into each muffin tin. Bake according to directions on cake mix. Ice cupcakes with your favorite frosting.

Bill & Phyllis Driggs at a King Family Christmas party

5-MINUTE CHOCOLATE MUG CAKE
(Tina Cole)

Really fun and yummy too! Great for 2 people, a small group or a kid's party. Wait- who am I kidding - adults love this too!

Per mug:
2 Tbsp. Hershey's Unsweetened Cocoa Powder
3 Tbsp. mini chocolate chips (optional, but best)
Vanilla ice cream or whipped cream
Splash of real vanilla extract
3 Tbsp. vegetable oil
4 Tbsp. flour
4 Tbsp. sugar
1 dash of salt
1 egg
3 Tbsp. milk

In a large coffee mug put flour, sugar, salt and cocoa powder and stir well. Add egg and beat well until just blended. Stir in milk, then oil and mix well. Add a splash of vanilla; stir well, then add mini chocolate chips and mix well but do not over-mix. Put the mug in the microwave (individually) and cook for 3 minutes at 1000 Watts (adjust accordingly if microwave has lower wattage.) The cake will rise over the top of the mug, but don't be alarmed! Allow to cool 1-2 min. and tip out onto a small plate. Top warm cake with whipped cream or ice cream. (For lower calories, use 1 tsp. oil instead of 3 Tbsp. oil plus one of the small cups of applesauce that come in a six-pack. Substitute Splenda for sugar - same amount)

If doing this with a group: line up all the ingredients on a counter with several mixing and measuring tablespoons (6 if you have them) and mugs for all. Then line up the people like an assembly line, and assign each one an ingredient or task to do for each mug (1 person does the flour, 1 does the sugar, 1 does the cocoa, 1 does the salt, 1 does the stirring, 1 does the egg, etc.) They put their ingredient in each mug going down the line. This is fun for kids and adults too!

CHOCOLATE TORTE
(Donna King Conkling)

Flourless cake

7oz. semi sweet chocolate bar
½ cup unsalted butter
7 eggs
¾ cup + ¼ cup sugar

⅛ tsp. cream of tartar
½ pint heavy cream
⅓ cup powdered sugar
2 tsp. vanilla

Preheat oven to 325°. Melt together 6 oz. chocolate (save 1 oz. for topping) and butter. Put aside. Separate 7 eggs. In large bowl beat yolks with ¾ cup sugar for 5 minutes. Gradually add chocolate mixture while warm into the egg yolks. Add 1 tsp. vanilla.

Beat together 7 egg whites and cream of tartar until peaks form. Add ¼ c. sugar slowly and beat more. Fold the egg whites carefully into the chocolate mixture. Pour ¾ of the batter into ungreased 9" spring form pan (put the remaining batter covered in refrigerator) and bake for 35 minutes. Cool cake. The center of the cake will drop as it cools. When cake has cooled completely, ice top with the remaining batter. Whip the heavy cream, powdered sugar, and 1 tsp. vanilla and frost the top of the cake. Use 1 oz. semi sweet chocolate to shave as a topping on the whipped cream.

CRANK KIDS BIRTHDAY FUNNEL CAKES
(Tina Cole)

At birthdays, I always let the kids make their own. They were very creative with their coils and squiggles.

Makes 10 (4") squiggles
Vegetable oil for frying
2 cups flour
1 Tbsp. sugar
¾ tsp. salt
1 tsp. double action baking powder
2 eggs slightly beaten
1 to 1 ¼ cups milk
Powdered sugar

Heat oil in heavy pot (should be a deep pot – not too wide.) Oil needs to be very hot, but not smoking. Combine dry ingredients in a medium mixing bowl. Make a well in the center. Pour eggs and 1 cup of milk into the well. Stir with large spoon until batter is smooth (adding more milk if batter is too thick to go through the funnel.) Ladle ½ cup of batter into a funnel, using fingertip to block hole and control flow. Dribble batter from funnel into center of hot oil, moving out in circles to make a snake-like coil of 3 or 4 rings. Deep fry about 2 minutes on each side – turning cake with a slotted spatula and tongs. Drain on thick paper towel then sprinkle liberally with powdered sugar.

VONNIE'S PIE CRUST
(Yvonne King Burch)

There is no better! You'll never want pie without this again! It has a unique texture and a great blend of flavors. You pat it into the pan so you don't have to roll it out! Many a family Thanksgiving pumpkin pie has this at the base of it.

Makes 8"-10" crust

1 ½ cup flour
1 tsp. salt
2 Tbsp. milk
1 tsp. sugar
½ cup oil

Mix flour, sugar and salt in a bowl. Mix oil and milk until blended and pour into dry mixture. Pat into pie plate. (You don't roll this crust out.) Bake 410° for 11-12 minutes for unfilled pie, or 10 minutes if filling the pie. If filled, cover the crust with foil.

STEVO'S LEMONADE ICE CREAM PIE
(Steve Driggs)

1 small can of frozen lemonade concentrate, totally thawed
1 half-gallon vanilla ice cream, softened
2 Oreo cookie pie crusts (regular size)
Toppings (see recipe)

Mix the thawed lemonade and softened ice cream together in a large mixing bowl until smooth and well mixed. Pour mixture into pie shells (will fill two pie shells). Add toppings if desired on top or mix in with ice cream, including fruit (strawberries, raspberries, etc.) or chocolate shavings, etc. Place in freezer over night. Let thaw a bit before serving. Makes a great summer desert.

PEACH COBBLER
(Chick Rey)

Serves 10

6 fresh peaches, cut up, mixed with 1 cup sugar
1 cup flour
2 eggs
1 tsp. baking powder
1 scant cup sugar
1 tsp. salt
2 Tbsp. butter
2 tsp. vanilla
¼ cup milk

Cook peaches in sugar in saucepan on low heat while preparing batter. Mix eggs, sugar, and butter together, then add milk, dry ingredients, and vanilla. Put batter in buttered and floured 9X13 baking dish, and pour hot peach mixture on top of batter. Bake at 375° for 30 min. Serve with vanilla ice cream or whipped cream or Half & Half or vanilla yogurt or whatever you like.

King Sister Luise with son Rob

CHOCOLATE ORANGE PIE
(Candy Brand)

Prepare a pie crust and set aside to cool.

Filling:

½ cup sugar	2 oz. unsweetened chocolate
3 Tbsp. cornstarch	2 egg yolks slightly beaten
¼ tsp. salt	2 Tbsp. butter
2 Tbsp. + 1 cup milk	½ tsp. vanilla

Orange topping:
1 tsp. unflavored gelatin
¼ cup powdered sugar
¼ cup frozen orange juice concentrate (thawed)
1 can mandarin oranges
1 cup heavy cream

In small bowl combine sugar, cornstarch, salt – mix well. Stir in 2 Tbsp. milk and set aside. In medium saucepan over low heat melt chocolate with 1 cup milk stirring constantly till smooth. Pour in and blend chocolate with cornstarch mixture in bowl. Cook low till thickens and boils 1 minute. Blend about ¼ cup hot mixture into egg yolks. Gradually stir yolks mixture into hot mixture in saucepan. Cook low 3 minutes stirring constantly. Remove from heat. Stir in butter and vanilla. Cover surface with plastic wrap and refrigerate until just cool – 1 hour. Spoon chocolate into pie shell.

Topping: In saucepan combine gelatin and OJ. Stir on low heat till gelatin dissolves. Cool slightly. In small bowl combine heavy cream and powdered sugar and beat to soft peaks. Fold OJ mixture into whipped cream. Spread over chocolate and refrigerate. Top with mandarin oranges dipped half way in melted chocolate.

CHOCOLATE SILK PIE
(Candy Brand, Noelle Sanderson)

1 pie crust	½ cup sugar
¼ cup cornstarch	⅛ tsp. salt
1 cup milk	3 oz. cream cheese, softened & cubed
2 egg yolks, beaten	6 oz. pkg. chocolate chips
1 ½ cups heavy cream	1 tsp. vanilla

In saucepan combine sugar, cornstarch and salt. Mix well and gradually stir in milk. Add chocolate chips and yolks. Cook over medium heat until mixture is thickened stirring constantly. This will take a while. Remove from heat. Stir in cream cheese and beat till smooth. Cover with plastic wrap and refrigerate for 1 hour. Beat whipping cream and vanilla. Reserve 1 cup for topping. Fold remaining cream into cooled chocolate mixture and spoon into cooled pie shell. I like Vonnie's Pie Crust for this. Refrigerate overnight to set.

Publicity photo of The Four King Cousins
(Candy, Carolyn, Cathy & Tina)

FRENCH HOT CHOCOLATE ICE CREAM PIE
(Marilyn King)

¼ cup sugar
3 egg yolks
1 ½ cups heavy cream
½ cup water
6 oz. chocolate chips
Graham cracker pie crust

In saucepan, mix sugar and water and boil rapidly for 3 minutes (makes syrup.) Mix in a blender chocolate chips and hot syrup until smooth. Add to the blender the egg yolks. Whip the cream and do not sweeten. Carefully fold in the whipped cream to the chocolate. Pour into a graham cracker crust. Cover with wax paper and freeze for 2-3 hours. Serve with more whipped cream and a dash of fresh raspberries.

CHOCOLATE MOUSSE PIE
(Debbie Fox)

1 pre-baked pie crust of your choice, 10" or deep dish plate
1 cup chocolate chips
8 oz. pkg. cream cheese, softened
1 pint heavy cream, whipped without sugar
2 Tbsp. sugar

Melt chocolate. Cream the cream cheese and sugar together; add the chocolate and blend. Add whipped cream and blend on low until well mixed. Put in crust and refrigerate. A great Thanksgiving alternate.

BROWNIE CHEESECAKE
(Laurette Walton)

Makes 12 brownies

Top	Bottom
8 oz. cream cheese	8 oz semi sweet chocolate squares
2 Tbsp. butter	4 Tbsp. butter
½ cup sugar	½ cup sugar
1 Tbsp. flour	2 eggs
2 eggs	1 tsp. vanilla
2 Tbsp. heavy cream	¼ tsp. almond extract
1 Tbsp. vanilla	½ tsp. salt

Cheesecake top:

Combine cream cheese and butter and beat till fluffy. Blend in sugar and flour. Add eggs, cream, vanilla, and beat till smooth. Set aside.

Brownie Bottom:

Melt chocolate squares in double boiler or microwave. Beat butter in mixer till fluffy. Beat in sugar and eggs slowly. Add vanilla, almond extract, salt, and chocolate into butter and eggs. Quickly blend in flour. Pour brownie into 9x13 pan. Slowly pour cheesecake on top of brownie and spread to make smooth. Bake 45 minutes in preheated 350° oven. Cool on rack and refrigerate.

CHICK'S CHEESECAKE
(Chick Rey)

Serves 8

FILLING

3 (8 oz) packages cream cheese
1 cup sugar
1 cup sour cream
1 tsp. vanilla
2 eggs
Pinch of salt

CRUST

12 large graham crackers
4 tsp. sugar
1 tsp. cinnamon
½ cup butter, melted

Mix filling in above order and set aside. For crust, crush graham crackers and add sugar, cinnamon, and butter. Grease round cake pan. Press graham cracker crumb mixture into bottom and sides of pan. Fill with cream cheese filling mixture. Bake at 350° for 35 minutes. Cool and chill. Serve topped with cherry, blueberry, or raspberry pie filling if desired. TIP: Melt butter in bottom of pan, then add crust, eliminating greasing the pan.

Alvino Rey & Kent Larsen in the Hollywood Christmas Parade

PEACH CARAMEL CHEESECAKE
(Laurette Walton)

Very special summertime dessert that looks beautiful and tastes amazing!

2 cups crushed shortbread cookies (about 28 cookies)
4 (8 oz) packages of cream cheese (softened)
½ cup small ripe peaches chopped (about one small peach)
5 cups thinly sliced fresh peaches (about 5-6 medium size)
¼ tsp. almond extract (optional but good)
¾ cup sugar
1 (5oz.) jar of caramel topping
1 (12oz.) jar of peach preserves
3 Tbsp. melted butter
3 Tbsp. heavy cream
1 tsp. vanilla
4 eggs

Combine cookie crumbs and butter and press into bottom and up sides of a greased 10 inch springform pan. Bake at 350° for 8 min. or until golden brown. Cool. Beat cream cheese at high speed with an electric mixer until creamy and smooth. Gradually add sugar, beating well. Add eggs, 1 at a time, beating well after each. Add extracts and pour into prepared crust in springform pan. Stir together caramel topping and heavy cream in a large glass bowl. Microwave on high 1-2 minutes, stirring once. Stir in chopped peaches. Then add peach mixture to cream cheese mixture and swirl gently. Bake 325° for 50 min. or until cheesecake is almost set. Turn off oven and let stand in oven with door partially open for 30 min more. Remove and cool on a wire rack. Cover and chill at least 8 hours. Release sides of pan and arrange sliced peaches in a swirl, covering the top of the cake. Microwave peach preserves in a glass bowl on high for 1-2 min. or until melted, stirring once.

Pour preserves through a wire mesh strainer into a bowl, then brush over sliced peaches.

DERBY PIE
(Laurette Walton)

The Kentucky Derby always runs the first Saturday in May. This is a traditional pie served during that time of year in Louisville where Laurette lived for awhile.

2 eggs slightly beaten
¾ cup sugar
¼ cup brown sugar
½ cup butter, melted & cooled
1 cup chopped pecans
1 cup chocolate chips
1 Tbsp. vanilla
9 inch unbaked pie crust

Combine all and pour into unbaked pie crust. Bake 350° for 45 minutes until set. Cool. Serve with vanilla ice cream or whipped cream.

Grandpa William King Driggs with the King kids on "The King Family Show" 1965

KEY LIME PIE
(Laurette Walton)

Crust:
1 ¼ cups graham cracker crumbs
¼ cup brown sugar
⅓ cup melted butter
Combine all ingredients and press into 9 inch pie plate. Bake at 375°, 6-8 minutes.

<u>Filling</u>
4 eggs, lightly beaten
1 cup sugar
Dash salt
⅛ cup grated lime zest
½ cup unsalted butter, softened
⅛ cup Key Lime Juice or fresh lime juice

<u>Topping</u>
1 cup heavy cream
⅓ cup powdered sugar
1 Tbsp. vanilla
lime slices

In a double boiler, combine all except butter. Bring water to a boil and reduce heat to low and cook, whisking constantly till thickened. Add butter, cook, whisking constantly until melts and is thick. Pour into cooled crust and bake at 300° for 20 minutes. Cool, cover and chill at least 8 hours. Before serving: whip heavy cream. Add powdered sugar and vanilla. Spread over cooled filling. Garnish with lime slices that are cut to center and twisted to make an "s" shape.

LEMON ANGEL PIE
(Donna King Conkling)

Served at many King Family summer parties. It's very cool and refreshing.

1 can Sweetened Condensed Milk
½ cup pure lemon juice
1 tsp. grated lemon zest
2 egg yolks, well beaten
1 pt. strawberries
Heavy cream, whipped and sweetened
1 pie crust

Mix together first 4 ingredients and pour into cooled pie shell. Chill in refrigerator until it sets. Top with halved strawberries and whipped cream on top.

PEANUT BUTTER CREAM PIE
(Brooke Smith)

4 oz. cream cheese
½ cup peanut butter (Jif recommended)
1 cup powdered sugar
Graham cracker crust
⅓ cup milk
9 oz. Cool Whip

Cream together cream cheese, powdered sugar, milk and peanut butter until smooth. Fold in Cool Whip. Pour into graham cracker or Oreo pie shell, bought or homemade. Chill for at least one hour.

BLUEBERRY CREAM PIE
(Laurette Walton)

Crust:
1 ¼ cups graham cracker crumbs
¼ cup sugar
⅓ cup melted butter
Mix and pat into pie pan. Do not bake.

Filling:
1 ½ cups heavy cream
Juice of 1 lemon
1 cup powdered sugar
8 oz. cream cheese, softened
1 can blueberry pie filling

Whip the cream for just a few seconds--then add lemon juice, powdered sugar, and cream cheese. Beat till firm. Pour into shell. Cover with blueberry pie filling. Refrigerate for several hours.

DONNA AND CAROLYN'S CHERRY CREAM PIE
(Donna Thomas, Carolyn Cameron)

1 (8 or 9 ") baked pie crust
8 oz. cream cheese, softened
1 can Sweetened Condensed Milk
1 tsp. vanilla
⅓ cup lemon juice
1 can cherry pie filling

Cream the cream cheese and slowly add condensed milk, stirring constantly so it doesn't get lumpy. Add vanilla and lemon juice. Stir quickly because lemon juice makes the mixture thicken. Pour into pie shell and refrigerate. When set, arrange pie cherries (I like the one with extra fruit) on top. Chill until ready to serve.

PEAR PIE

(Yvonne King Burch)

Must start with Vonnie's Pie Crust! And, as Vonnie points out, be sure to top this with whipped cream. The King Family wouldn't think of having pie without it.

Filling:
In a blender put:

2 eggs	1 cup sugar
½ cup butter, melted	4 Tbsp. flour
Nutmeg and cinnamon to taste	5-6 fresh pears

Boil water and place pears in just long enough to loosen skins. Peel them. Cut strips lengthwise through the pear and place pears in a pinwheel design (oh yes, make it "Vonnie" beautiful). Pour blended mixture SLOWLY over pears so it seeps through. Bake 350° for 60-70 minutes or until golden and dry looking. Serve with whipped cream.

The King Sisters pose in front of the Steel Pier marquee

PUMPKIN CHIFFON PIE
(Xan Albright)

This is a delicious alternate to regular pumpkin pie—always gets rave reviews!

9-10" pie shell (Vonnie's Pie Crust is the best! – See recipe)
2 (3 oz.) pkg. vanilla instant pudding (can use sugar free)
1 ½ tsp. pumpkin pie spice
1 can (16 oz.) pumpkin
9 oz. Cool Whip
1 ⅓ cups milk
Pecans (optional)

Add pudding mix to milk and mix with beater 30 seconds. Blend in pumpkin, spice, 2 cups of the Cool Whip. Put all in pie crust. Chill at least 4 hours. Top with remaining Cool Whip and pecan halves.

King Cousins on the set of the 2009 public television special "Christmas with the King Family"
back: Xan, Cathy, Tina, Candy | *front*: Jamie, Ric, Cam, Susannah

FRENCH MINT PIE
(Donna King Conkling)

Crust:
1 ½ cups crushed vanilla wafers
⅓ cup butter, melted
Make pie shell and bake at 350° for 10 minutes.

Filling:
1 cup powdered sugar
½ cup butter
2 squares unsweetened chocolate, melted
2 eggs beaten
3 drops oil of peppermint
½ pint heavy cream, whipped and lightly sweetened

Cream sugar and butter, added melted chocolate. Add eggs and continue mixing till fluffy. Add flavoring and chill overnight. Serve very cold, with sweetened whipped cream.

CUSTARD DESSERT
(Yvonne King Burch)

4 cups scalded milk   ¼ tsp. salt
6 eggs slightly beaten   1 tsp. vanilla
1 cup sugar

In a 1 ½ quart Pyrex buttered bowl, beat eggs and add the rest. (Pour scalded milk through a strainer first.) Mix all. Sprinkle with nutmeg. Place bowl inside larger pan filled 1 ½ inches deep with water. Bake 315° degrees 50-60 minutes, knife will come out dry. On top serve an exotic fruit like mango or berries and whipped cream.

SHERBET AND FRUIT MOUND
(Donna King Conkling)

Various sherbet containers
Various fresh fruit

In large bowl that can fit in your freezer, scoop with ice cream scooper the following sherbets until you've filled up the bowl or have enough to serve how ever many guests you have: pineapple, raspberry, lime, orange.

Put in freezer. Just before serving, take out of freezer and pile the scoops into a large mound on a large serving dish or bowl.

Add the following to the top and all around the sherbet:

Strawberries	Sprigs of mint	Purple Grapes
Raspberries	Bananas	Pecans
Boysenberries	Blueberries	

HOMEMADE FRUIT ICE CREAM
(Xan Albright)

Makes 2 quarts

1 quart milk
1 pint Half & Half
1 pint heavy cream
3 cups sugar
1 small can OJ, undiluted
¾ cup lemon juice
3 mashed bananas
2 cups crushed pineapple, drained
1 cup raspberries

Mix all the milks/creams together with the sugar. Add the remaining ingredients. Put in ice cream maker and freeze.

HOMEMADE VANILLA PUDDING ICE CREAM
(Donna King Conkling)

Makes 1 gallon

½ pint heavy cream
1 quart of Half & Half
1 small pkg. vanilla instant pudding
3 ½ cups sugar
3 quarts whole milk
3 Tbsp. vanilla extract

Whip up heavy cream until fluffy or foamy. Add Half & Half, vanilla pudding, sugar and vanilla. Add milk to fill freezer pan and freeze. You can make strawberry or peach ice cream by reducing milk and adding 3 cups of crushed fruit with 2 tsp. of lemon juice.

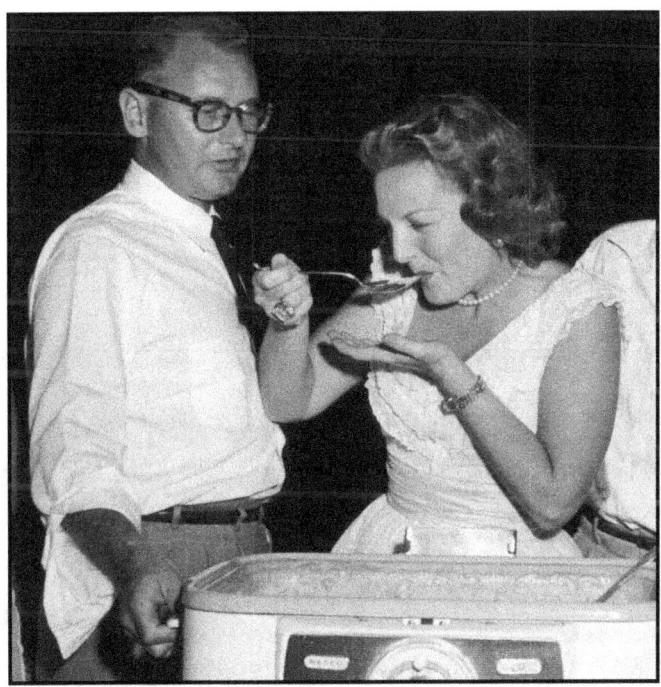

Donna & brother Bill taste-testing in 1958

"RICHIE KING" CLARKE'S FABULOUS HOMEMADE VANILLA ICE-CREAM

(Ric de Azevedo)

This is so simple but tastes so good. Anyone who knows Ric knows that he is a chocoholic, but this vanilla ice cream is so good you do not want to put toppings on it. It only hides the taste.

Makes 1 gallon
3 quarts heavy cream
3 cups granulated sugar
Real Vanilla from Mexico
⅛ tsp. salt

Now for the good part. Most recipes call for about 3 or 4 tsp. vanilla. I say, triple that or more. I use over ¼ to ☐ cup of Real Mexican Vanilla; don't substitute any other kind. Mix all of the ingredients with a wisk until all of the sugar dissolves. No cooking, just pour into ice cream container. Follow your ice cream maker's instructions for churning. Remove "dasher" from ice cream container, eat all the ice cream off of the "dasher" and put ice cream container in the freezer. Incredible! Remember - no toppings.

Ric on graduation day in his new red 1964 Pontiac GTO

HOMEMADE CHOCOLATE ICE CREAM
(Lorie Albright)

½ cup cocoa powder
2 ½ cup Half & Half
1 ½ cups heavy cream
1 heaping cup of sugar
9 egg yolks
2 tsp. vanilla

In a saucepan, slowly pour, mixing as you do, the Half & Half and heavy cream into the cocoa powder. Heat on medium heat to a simmer; remove from heat.

Beat yolks in a bowl until light yellow. Add the sugar, continuing to beat on low. Slowly add chocolate cream to the eggs. Place this mixture into the saucepan, heating on low. Stir often, and cook until slightly thickened and coats the back of your spoon. Pour mixture into a bowl, add vanilla, and let it rest for 20 min. Cool in frig. When it's cold, pour it into your ice cream maker and process according to directions for ice cream (about 30 min.) If you want it get to harder, put it into a new container and freeze. Fabulous, rich chocolate ice cream!

The King Sisters perform on "The King Family Show" 1965

FUDGE-TOPPED BROWNIES
(Carla Rey, Candy Brand)

Makes 2-3 dozen

1 cup butter or margarine, melted
2 eggs
3 tsp. vanilla
⅔ cup cocoa
1 cup nuts, chopped
2 cup white sugar
½ cup milk
1 cup flour
½ tsp. baking powder

Frosting:
12 oz. pkg. semi-sweet chocolate chips
1 can (14 oz.) sweetened condensed milk

Alternate frosting: (Cream all ingredients together)
8 oz. cream cheese, softened
1 box powdered sugar
1 tsp. vanilla
⅓-½ cup cocoa powder
⅓ cup chocolate syrup
½ cup butter, softened

Mix together melted butter and sugar. Add eggs, milk, 1 ½ tsp. vanilla and mix. Add flour, cocoa, and baking powder and beat well. Stir in nuts. Spread into 9x13 greased Pyrex and bake at 350° for 40 minutes. Just before the brownies are finished, melt the chocolate chips with the condensed milk and remaining vanilla (or make alternate frosting). Remove from heat and spread this over the hot cooked brownies. Chill completely.

OATMEAL SCOTCHIES
(Donna Thomas)

Makes 4 dozen cookies

1 cup butter or Crisco
1 ½ cup firmly packed brown sugar
2 eggs
1 Tbsp. water
2 cups flour
2 tsp. baking powder
1 tsp. baking soda
1 tsp. salt
1 ½ cups quick oats
6 oz. butterscotch chips
1 tsp. orange extract

Combine shortening/butter, brown sugar, eggs and water. Beat until creamy. Sift together; flour, baking powder, soda and salt. Add to creamy mixture. Stir in oats, chips and orange extract. Drop by tablespoonfuls onto cookie sheets. Bake at 375° for 10 - 12 minutes.

Del Courtney, Bob Clarke & LaVarn Thomas at rehearsals for a King Family concert

LEMON DROP COOKIES

(Xan Albright)

People can't quite figure out what's in these, but they absolutely die for them! Perfect to serve at a bridal or baby shower.

Makes 100 small cookies

1 ½ cups butter flavored Crisco
4 cups flour
1 ½ tsp. baking powder
1 ½ tsp. baking soda
1 tsp. salt
2 cups sugar
3 eggs
2 tsp. vanilla
1 tsp. lemon extract
Zest of one lemon
6 oz. lemon drop candies, crushed

Glaze:
1 cup powdered sugar
Juice of 1 lemon

Blend dry ingredients. Cream sugar, Crisco, eggs, vanilla, lemon extract and zest. Add crushed lemon drops. Mix well. Roll 1-2" dough balls with your hands and place on cookie sheet covered with parchment paper. Flatten cookies slightly with a glass dipped in sugar and bake at 350° for 8-10 minutes. Cool for 3 minutes, then remove to cooling rack and spread glaze over, using a pastry brush.

CHOCOLATE MINT COOKIES
(Xan Albright)

Makes 75 small cookies

2 cups chocolate chips, melted
¾ cup margarine
1 ½ cups brown sugar
2 Tbsp. water
2 eggs
2 ½ cups flour
½ tsp. salt
1 ¼ tsp. baking soda
35 Andes Mints, unwrapped and cut in half

After melting chocolate chips, mix everything together except the Andes Mints. Chill for 1 hour. Roll into balls with hands and put on ungreased cookie sheet. Bake at 350° for 10-12 minutes (ready when top is crackled). As soon as you remove from oven, put the ½ Andes mint on top. As it starts to melt, spread in circular motion with knife. (These are great served with Lemon Drop Cookies.)

"Thanksgiving with the King Family" TV special 1967

NO BAKE PEANUTTY CHOCOLATE DROPS
(Donna King Conkling)

Makes 4 dozen

½ cup butter or margarine
½ cup unsweetened cocoa
14 oz. can Sweetened Condensed Milk
2 ½ cups Quick cooking oats
1 cup peanuts, chopped
½ cup peanut butter

Line baking sheets with waxed or parchment paper. In medium saucepan over medium heat, melt butter and stir in cocoa. Bring mixture to a boil, stirring constantly. Remove from heat, stir in remaining ingredients. Drop by teaspoonfuls onto prepared baking sheets. Let set in refrigerator.

YUMMY SQUARES
(Jamie Miller)

A favorite Conkling cousin treat which Jamie could always whip up in just minutes...to all our delights!

Makes 2 dozen

12 large rectangles of graham crackers, crushed
¼ cup butter, melted
1 (12 oz.) pkg. chocolate chips
1 cup walnuts (optional)
1 can Eagle brand Sweetened Condensed Milk

Mix all together. Put in lightly greased or buttered 9x9 (or 7x11) pan. Bake at 350° for 20-25 minutes or until golden brown.

MILK CHOCOLATE BUTTERSCOTCH CAFÉ COOKIES
(Erin Arnett)
Scrumdiddlyumptious!

Makes 2-3 dozen

1 (18 oz.) pkg. Pillsbury Refrigerated Sugar Cookies
1/3 cup firmly packed brown sugar
1 tsp. vanilla
¾ cup oatmeal
½ cup butterscotch chips
2 (1.55 oz.) milk chocolate candy bars, finely chopped

Spray cookie sheets with nonstick cooking spray. Break up sugar cookie dough into a large bowl. Add brown sugar and vanilla; mix well. Add oats, chips and chocolate; mix well. Dough will be stiff. Bake at 350° for 13-18 min, or until cookies are golden brown. Cool 1 minute. Remove from cookie sheet.

PEANUT BUTTER BLOSSOM COOKIES
(Laurette Walton)

Makes 3 dozen

½ cup butter
½ cup brown sugar
½ cup sugar
½ cup peanut butter
1 egg
2 Tbsp. milk
2 tsp. vanilla
1 ¾ cups flour
1 tsp. baking soda
½ tsp. salt
Hershey's Kisses

Cream butter, sugars, peanut butter, egg, milk and vanilla. Add flour, baking soda, and salt. Mix well. Roll 1 inch balls of dough and roll them in sugar. Bake for 8 minutes. Take out of the oven and place a Hershey's Kiss in the center. Bake for 1-2 additional minutes.

PUMPKIN BARS
(Laurette Walton, Amy Nottingham)

Wonderful in the fall

4 eggs	Frosting:
1 2/3 cups sugar	8 oz. cream cheese
1 cup oil	¼ cup butter
16 oz. can solid pack pumpkin	2 cups powdered sugar
2 cups flour	1 tsp. vanilla
2 tsp. cinnamon	Milk, if needed
2 tsp. baking powder	
1 tsp. baking soda	
1 tsp. salt	

In a large bowl combine eggs, sugar, oil, and pumpkin; mix well. Add flour, cinnamon, baking powder, baking soda, and salt; mix well. Pour into a 15x10x1 (or larger) pan. Bake at 350°F for about 25 minutes. Cool and add frosting.

Debbie, Cam & Laurette backstage at a King Family concert

DELUXE LEMON BARS
(Shauna Elliott)

2 cups + ¼ cup sifted flour
½ cup sifted powdered sugar
½ tsp. baking powder
2 cups sugar
4 eggs
1 cup butter
⅓ cup lemon juice

Sift together the 2 cups of the flour and powdered sugar. Cut the butter into the mixture until it all clings together. Press into 9x13 pan, up the sides as well. Bake at 350° for 20-25 minutes until lightly brown. Beat the eggs, sugar, and lemon juice together in a small bowl. Sift together the remaining ¼ cup flour and baking powder. Add it to the egg mixture. Pour over the baked crust and bake at 350° another 25 minutes. Top should be slightly crusted and lemon filling will be soft.

MAGIC COOKIE BARS
(Chris Conkling)

No mix, no fuss, no mess! This is fun for kids to make.

Makes 2 dozen
½ cup butter or margarine
1 ½ cups graham cracker crumbs
1 (14oz.) can of sweetened condensed milk
6 oz. semi sweet chocolate chips
1 cup chopped nuts
1 (3 ½ oz.) flaked coconut

In 9x13 baking pan, melt butter. Sprinkle crumbs over butter; pour sweetened condensed milk evenly over crumbs. Top evenly with remaining ingredients; press down gently. Bake 350° for 25-40 minutes. Cool.

CHOCOLATE CHIP PUDDING COOKIES
(Ray Driggs)

Makes 4 dozen

1 small box vanilla instant pudding and pie filling
2 cups unsifted flour
1 cup butter (soft)
¾ cup light brown sugar
12 oz. pkg. chocolate chips
1 tsp. baking soda
¼ cup sugar
1 tsp. vanilla
2 eggs

Mix flour, vanilla pudding powder mix, and baking soda in one bowl. In a separate bowl mix the butter, sugars, vanilla, and eggs. Beat until smooth and creamy. Add dry mixture slowly. You may need to add just a little milk to keep it from being too dry. Add chocolate chips. Drop by rounded teaspoonfuls on ungreased cookie sheets, about 2 inches apart. Bake at 375° for about 8 to 9 min. Let cool.

THE ULTIMATE SUGAR COOKIE
(Annie Wilkins)
These melt in your mouth and are so easy to make!

Makes 4 dozen

2 ½ cups flour
¼ tsp. baking soda
1 cup sugar
3 Tbsp. heavy cream
½ tsp. salt
½ cup butter, softened
2 eggs
1 tsp. vanilla

Combine flour, salt, and soda in a bowl. Mix butter, sugar, and eggs. Stir in cream and vanilla. Add in flour mix. Mix well and chill for 5 hours. Roll dough onto floured board to ½ inch thickness. Cut out cookies and place on a baking sheet. Bake at 400° for 6-8 min. Let stand before removing from sheet. Cool for 30 minutes, then frost with your favorite frosting.

ANGEL SUGAR COOKIES
(Laurette Walton)

The absolute best-tasting cookies but so delicate you can't cut them into shapes

Makes 5-6 dozen

1 cup butter
1 cup oil
1 cup sugar
1 cup powdered sugar
1 Tbsp. cream of tartar
2 eggs
4 cups flour
1 Tbsp. baking soda
1 Tbsp. salt

Frosting:
3-4 cups powdered sugar
½ cup butter
3 Tbsp. milk
Pinch of salt
1 Tbsp. vanilla
1 Tbsp. vanilla

Cream together first 4 ingredients. Add cream of tartar and eggs. Then add flour, soda, salt, and vanilla. Drop spoonfuls of dough into a bowl of sugar. Lightly shape into balls. Flatten with glass. Bake 8-10 minutes at 350° until very slightly golden brown on edges. Cool. Frost with homemade butter cream icing and decorate. You can freeze these cookies too.

YUMMY SHORTBREAD COOKIES WITH JAM
(Wendy Moran)

Makes 3 dozen

1 cup granulated sugar
1 cup unsalted butter, room temp
1 egg
1 tsp. vanilla or almond extract (either is good)
1½ cups flour
½ tsp. salt
1 cup flaked coconut
1 cup very finely chopped pecans
1 jar seedless raspberry jam (or other flavor if you like)

Cream together sugar, butter, egg and vanilla. Add flour and salt and mix well. Fold in coconut and pecans. Shape into 1" balls, place on an ungreased cookie sheet, and gently press a small hole in the top with your thumb. Place a small dollop of jam in the hole (too much will melt out over the side of the cookie.) Bake at 325° for 10-15 minutes until just slightly golden around edges. Cool.

Original King Sister Maxine with her husband LaVarn Thomas in Woodland Hills, CA

COCONUT CRUNCH CHOCOLATE CHIP COOKIES
(Laurette Walton)
So chewy and moist they last for days!

Makes 4 ½ dozen

1½ cups flour	1 cup brown sugar
1 tsp. baking powder	2 eggs
1 tsp. baking soda	1 tsp. vanilla
1 tsp. salt	2 cups oatmeal
½ cup butter	2 cups Rice Krispies
½ cup shortening	1 cup coconut
1 cup sugar	2 ½ cups chocolate chips

Measure dry ingredients and set aside. Beat butter, shortening and sugars in large bowl. Add eggs, one at a time, then vanilla. Gradually add flour mixture. Stir in oats, Rice Krispies, coconut, and chocolate chips. Form balls with 2 Tbsp. of dough. Bake at 350° for 10 min.

CARMELITAS
(Laurette Walton)

Makes 3 dozen

2 cups butter	2 ¼ cups brown sugar
3 cups flour	3 cups quick oats
1 Tbsp. salt	2 Tbsp. baking soda
1 jar caramel sauce	1 (16oz.) pkg. chocolate chips

Soften butter and mix it with all dry ingredients. Pat ¾ of the batter in large jellyroll pan. Bake 350° for 8-10 minutes. Cool 10 minutes. Pour caramel sauce and chocolate chips on top. Sprinkle the rest of batter of top of chips. Bake another 10-12 minutes. Cut into squares. This recipe can be cut in half and put in a 9x13 pan.

PEARL'S DIVINITY
(Grandma Pearl Driggs)

Grandma Pearl made this recipe every Christmas and Easter for more than 40 years and became famous for it. Her grandchildren can recall the smooth, white divinity, laid out on wax paper, nearly covering her entire table. Her two daughters, Donna and Yvonne, tell their version of how Pearl made the recipe in their own particular vernacular.

Makes 3 - 4 dozen pieces

Do not make this recipe on a rainy day; it has to be good weather. The difference between Pearl's Divinity and other recipes was her use of dark syrup. Vonnie claims it's best to make this with two people.

4 cups sugar
1 cup cold water
1 cup dark Karo syrup
4 egg whites, beaten very stiff
Walnuts

Cook sugar, water, and Karo syrup until it boils, then simmer. Keep simmering until it reaches a "hard ball stage." (This means when you place a drop of syrup in a cup of cold water, the syrup will form a hard ball [not soft ball like in hot fudge]). You should also be able to pick up the hard ball and "tinkle" it (which means when you "plink" it against the cup edge, it will "ting" and make a tinkling sound.)

Remove from heat. Pour the syrup very slowly into the very stiff egg whites as you are beating with an electric beater. (One person can pour syrup, the other beats the egg mixture.) Beat until the beater can't move anymore because the candy has become so thick. Take the beater out and continue to beat by hand until the mixture shows a grain (like the sugary grain you might see in fudge). If you do not reach the grainy stage, your candy will go flat. Spoon candy onto wax paper and top immediately with a walnut half. If it looks flat, take the walnuts off and beat it some more!

Note: Only Donna and Vonnie talk in parentheses-within-parentheses type sentences! Can't you just hear them trying to explain it, interrupting each other every step of the way?

WHITE CHOCOLATE CRUNCH
(Xan Albright)
Be careful – you may eat the entire bowl!

Fills a large serving bowl
2 cups pretzels (I use mini pretzels)
2 cups Chex cereal
1 cup nuts – your choice, (but honey roasted peanuts or cashews are divine)
½ pkg. sliced almonds
35 caramels cut into fourths
12 oz. pkg white chocolate chips

Toast the almonds in the oven a few minutes on a cookie sheet. Cool. In a large bowl mix together everything except the white chocolate. Melt the chocolate chips in a double boiler and pour over all the ingredients. Mix well. Spread out onto a cookie sheet covered with parchment paper. When cooled, break into bite-sized pieces.

ENGLISH TOFFEE
(Candy Brand)

Makes a bowlful

8 oz chocolate bar (or choc. chips)
1 cup butter
1 cup margarine
6 Tbsp. water
2 cups sugar
2 tsp. vanilla
¾ cup pecans, chopped

In heavy saucepan, melt butter and margarine. Add water and sugar. Bring to a boil and then take off the stove, covering it with a lid. Let it rest for 10 min. While you wait, cut up chocolate bar (or use chocolate chips). Spread chocolate pieces and pecans on a baking sheet. Reheat "rested" sugar/butter mixture over medium heat, stirring constantly until it turns a golden brown (10-20 min). It actually will start to smoke a bit and smell almost burnt, but that is when it will reach the golden brown stage. Add vanilla and pour mixture over the chocolate and nuts. Cool and break up.

**Rehearsing the 'Mother-Daughter Medley' on
"The King Family Show" 1965**

MICROWAVE PEANUT BRITTLE
(Xan Albright)
This tastes as good as See's!

½ cup light corn syrup
1 cup sugar
1 cup dry roasted peanuts, cashews, pecans, or almonds
1 tsp. soft margarine
1 tsp. vanilla
1 tsp. baking soda

Combine corn syrup and sugar in 1½ or 2 qt. microwave round dish (not a disposable kind, but a sturdy kind). Stir well until evenly blended. Microwave on high for 4 minutes. Stir in nuts. Microwave on high for 3 minutes until light brown. Stir in margarine and vanilla and blend. Microwave on high for 1-2 minutes. Add baking soda and stir gently, just until light and foamy. Quickly pour onto lightly greased baking sheet. Cool and then break up into pieces. (This really works!) Note: for clear brittle, omit the baking soda.

Multiple generations of King Cousins & friends at rehearsals for a benefit concert in 2005

MUDDIE BUDDIES
(Jani Driggs)

Makes 10-12 cups
1 cups semi-sweet chocolate chips
9 cups CHEX cereal
½ cup peanut butter
¼ cup margarine
1 tsp. vanilla
1 ½ cup powdered sugar

Pour cereal into a large bowl. Melt chips, peanut butter, and margarine in bowl (microwave-safe bowl if you want to melt in microwave). Stir in vanilla. Pour chocolate mixture over cereal, stirring until coated. Pour this mixture into a large Ziploc bag. Pour powdered sugar into bag, seal bag, and shake until mixture is well coated. Hint: It helps to put half the powdered sugar in the bag first, then add mixture, then add other half of powdered sugar on top.

A family picnic with new generations of King Cousins

King Cousins Jamie, Carolyn, Cathy & Tina perform with John Davidson on "The Kraft Summer Music Hall" in 1966

Beverages, Dips, Sauces & Appetizers

The girl cousins on the set of the 1971 TV Special "The King Family in San Francisco"

JIM CONKLING'S FAMOUS EGG NOG
(Jim Conkling)

This was served every year at Donna and Jim's Christmas "fireside" parties completely filled with family and dear friends

For a blender recipe that serves 6:
(multiply for whatever size crowd you are serving)
3 cups Egg Nog, regular or low-fat (so buy a quart)
1 pint heavy cream, whipped and sweetened
1 cup milk – 1% or 2%
1 cup crushed ice
Nutmeg for topping

In a blender add egg nog and milk (I use 3 parts egg nog to 1 part milk.) Add crushed ice. Blend until frothy. Pour into punch bowl. Drop dollops of sweetened whipped cream on top and sprinkle with nutmeg. People love it because it is so cold and frothy!

HOT HOLIDAY CIDER
(Carolyn Cameron, Tina Cole)

We make this on Halloween night and keep it going until New Years, just refreshing it from time to time. It leaves a heavenly scent throughout the house.

Serves 15

1 qt apple juice	¼ cup honey
1 qt cranberry juice	3-4 cinnamon sticks
1 cup orange juice	Apple slices, horizontally cut
¼ cup lemon juice	1 tsp. nutmeg
2 tsp. cinnamon	½ tsp. whole cloves

Put everything in a Crockpot and heat. Add more juices and spices as you need to refill. The older it gets, the better it gets.

GOURMET HOT CHOCOLATE
(Donna King Conkling, Yvonne King Burch)

Serves 12
2 ½ sq. unsweetened baking chocolate
½ cups water
1 tsp. salt
1 tsp. vanilla
2 tsp. butter
¾ cups granulated sugar
½ pint heavy cream
½ gallon milk

Put chocolate and water in pan and cook over low heat, stirring constantly for 5 minutes until smooth and thick. Add salt, vanilla, butter and granulated sugar. Bring just to a boil 4 min stir constantly, remove heat and cool. Whip the cream until stiff. Fold into chocolate mixture and refrigerate. Scald but do not boil milk.

To serve: Put chocolate whipped cream in big, lovely crystal bowl and hot milk in silver pitcher for an elegant look. Place 2 - 3 heaping tablespoons of chocolate mixture into teacup or mug. Pour hot milk into the cup of chocolate mixture. Stir and serve.

FROSTY, ZESTY PARTY PUNCH
(Candy Brand)
Great for a big party or divide in thirds for a smaller gathering

Serves 150

Juice from 6 fresh lemons

3 (12 oz) cans frozen orange juice

18 cups water

3 (12 oz) cans lemonade concentrate

3 (46 oz) cans pineapple juice

12 cups sugar

8 liters lemon-lime soda or Ginger Ale

Mix thoroughly until frozen concentrates have thawed and sugar has dissolved. Freeze in gallon containers (Tupperware or cut-off plastic milk containers.) Before serving, thaw frozen mixture for 30-45 minutes. Mix with lemon-lime soda or Ginger Ale, one liter per gallon of frozen mix. Divide all ingredients into thirds for a smaller recipe.

MAXINE'S BEST PUNCH EVER
(Maxine King Thomas)

Serves 20-30

1 large can pineapple juice

1 small can lemonade

1¼ cup apricot nectar

1 large ginger ale

Mix, add ice, and serve.

LIME CUCUMBER PUNCH
(Stefanie Heaton)

Serves 20
2 - (2 Liter) bottles of lemon/lime soda
1 (12 oz. can) frozen limeade concentrate
1 cucumber thinly sliced in rounds
("English" cucumber is best if you can find it)
Bag of ice cubes

Add frozen limeade to soda and mix together. Add ice to serve very cold. Float cucumbers on top for flavor, decoration, and to eat if desired. Very refreshing drink!

FRESH FRUIT LEMONADE
(Jennifer Suttner)

Serves 6-8
Approximately 6 lemons
Zest of 4 lemons
4 cups water
1 cup sugar
½ cup fresh blackberries, raspberries, or strawberries

Squeeze enough lemon juice to make 1 cup. Add zest of 4 lemons. Boil water and dissolve sugar in it. Add the zest and lemon juice. Puree fruit in a blender and add to the lemonade. Pour through a sieve and chill. Garnish with lemon slices and mint leaves.

FRUIT DIP
(Cheryl Driggs)

Dip 1:
1 jar marshmallow crème
8 oz. soft cream cheese
Pinch of ginger
1 Tbsp. orange rind

Dip 2:
1 jar marshmallow crème
1 container strawberry cream cheese

Simply mix the ingredients together and chill. Serve with fruit tray.

THE BEST GUACAMOLE SAUCE IN TOWN
(Jamie Miller)

This was served with taquitos at many family parties over the years.

Makes about 2 cups
14 oz can tomatillos
1 lg. avocado
2 yellow peppers (canned)
2 large or 4 medium garlic cloves
½ tsp. salt

Drain tomatillos. Combine all ingredients in the blender.

HOT ARTICHOKE DIP
(Tina Cole, Jennifer Howard)

Enough dip for 20-30 people
8 oz. cream cheese, whipped or softened
2 (14 oz) jars marinated artichoke hearts, chopped
1 small can mild chopped green chilies
1 ½ cups grated Parmesan cheese
½ cup onion, finely chopped
1 cup grated Jack cheese
8 oz. sour cream
1 cup mayo
Pepper

Blend together cream cheese, mayo, and sour cream. Drain artichokes and chilies and add to mixture. Add onions, jack cheese, dash of pepper, and ½ of the Parmesan cheese. Pour into buttered baking dish – 10" cake pan, 9 x13, or large hollowed-out bread loaf (to make bowl.) Sprinkle with remaining Parmesan cheese and dot with butter. Bake in pre-heated 350° oven for 20 minutes. Then put under broiler for 5 minutes.

Variations:
You can add one, some, or all of the following ingredients by mixing them into the dip before baking:
* 1 pkg. slivered almonds
* ½ jar sun dried tomatoes in oil, chopped
* 1 jar Armour dried beef, chopped
* 1 small can French's French Fried Onions – ½ mixed in and ½ for topping (reserve ½ the can to sprinkle on top before putting in the broiler)
Serve hot with tortilla chips or torn chunks of bread from the bread bowl.

GREG'S SALSA

(Xan Albright)

Everyone requests this as a Christmas gift!

Makes 1 quart of salsa

4 - 6 (14 oz) cans diced tomatoes
2 yellow hat peppers
2 jalapeno peppers
1 bunch green onions, sliced
½ bunch chopped parsley
1 bunch chopped cilantro
Salt to taste

Put in blender: 1 can tomatoes and cut up peppers. Liquify. Mix with rest of ingredients in bowl. Put in fridge to "season."

ROB'S GUACAMOLE

(Laurette Walton)

Serves 8

5-6 ripe avocados
Juice of one lime
1-2 cloves fresh garlic, minced
Lawry's and pepper to taste

Mash avocados with fork. Add remaining ingredients and adjust until it tastes right. You can use as many avocados as you want and just add more lime and seasonings. Add some cut up pickled jalapenos (from a jar) if you want it to have a good kick.

BAKED BEAN DIP
(Laurette Walton)

This is a dip that my Aunt Vonnie gave me for my wedding shower. If the truth be known, though, she borrowed it from her daughter, Tina's, TV mother-in-law turned real life mother-in-law, Beverly Garland.

Serves 10-12

2 (10 1/2 oz.) cans of Frito Lay Bean Dip
20 drops Tabasco sauce
1 cup sour cream
1 bunch green onion, chopped
8 oz. package cream cheese
½ lb ea. grated cheddar and Monterey Jack cheese
1 envelope taco seasoning

Mix everything together (except grated cheese). Pour into shallow ungreased 8X8 casserole. Then add grated cheese on top. Bake 15 min. at 350°. Serve with tortilla chips.

Laurette at a costume fitting for "The King Family Show" with legendary designer Bob Mackie

FABULOUS NO-GOOF SAUCES
(Tina Cole)

BLENDER HOLLANDAISE:
1 cup butter (2 cubes)
4 egg yolks 2 Tbsp. lemon juice
¼ tsp. salt
¼ tsp. Tabasco

Heat butter in small pan until very hot. Put egg yolks, Tabasco, lemon juice, and salt in blender. Turn blender on low speed for 5 seconds. Slowly pour in hot butter in a steady stream. Turn off blender (add tsp. hot water if too thick).

BLENDER BÉARNAISE:
¼ cup white wine
2 Tbsp. tarragon vinegar
1 tsp. tarragon leaves
1 Tbsp. chopped shallots
¼ tsp. ground pepper

Leave Hollandaise Sauce (above) in blender. Combine all "Béarnaise" ingredients in small saucepan. Bring to boil until reduced to 3 Tbsp. Then add to Hollandaise Sauce in blender. Blend on low speed 30 seconds, and then turn on high for 8 seconds.

Tina, Vonnie, Kent, LaVarn, Maxine, Marilyn, Cathy, Donna, Candy & Alyce In the kitchen preparing for dinner

CINNAMON SCENTED CRANAPPLE SAUCE
(Jennifer Suttner)

Great to serve with pork chops, pork tenderloin or Thanksgiving turkey.

Serves 10-12

1 (16oz.) can whole berry cranberry sauce
1 (15oz.) can cinnamon flavored pear halves, drained and chopped
1 (11oz.) can mandarin oranges, drained
1 Granny Smith apple, peeled and chopped
1 cup sugar

Combine all ingredients in a large saucepan. Cook uncovered over medium/low heat 45 minutes, stirring often. Cover and chill.

King Sister Alyce with sons Ric & Lex at a King Family party

ROSE'S SAUCE
(Laurette Walton)

We use this over tortellini--but I also think it would make a delicious cream of tomato soup!

Serves 6-8

½ cup butter	3 Tbsp. chopped onion
3 Tbsp. chopped celery	3 Tbsp. chopped carrot
2 tsp. salt	½ tsp. sugar
Pepper	Italian seasons
Lawry's	½ -1 cup heavy cream

2 ½ cups canned tomatoes (Italian) with juice (large can 28 oz.)

Put everything but cream in saucepan and simmer for 1 hour. Puree contents in blender but leave a little texture. Put back in saucepan and return to simmer. Add heavy cream (start with ½ cup and add to taste), adjust seasonings and cook for a few minutes until heated through.

BARBEQUE SAUCE
(Candy Brand)

Recipe for 10 lbs. of meat

1 lg. bottle Ketchup	1 Tbsp. Worcestershire sauce
¼ cup vinegar	2 Tbsp. soy sauce
¼ onion, chopped	¼ cup Coke
¼ cup brown sugar	1 Tbsp. dry mustard

Marinade all night.

The King Family loves to entertain. Guests, welcomed by the sound of "background mood music" playing, can always head straight to a cozy table laden with appetizers, which always includes the family staple of Triscuits and WisPride Cheese.

BLUE CHEESE BALLS
(Erin Arnett)
Great for a holiday gift for friends

Makes 3 balls
3 (8 oz.) pkgs. cream cheese
3 (8 oz.) pkgs. WisPride soft cheese or other soft cheese in a container
½ pkg. Laura Scudder's blue cheese dressing mix
2 tsp. minced dry onion

Soften cheese to room temperature. Blend all ingredients with mixer. Roll in saran wrap and store in bowl with rounded bottom. Next Day: Roll in chopped nuts. Wrap in saran wrap and store. Makes 3 large cheese balls; can be frozen for a long time!

"MIXED UP" CHEESE BALL
(Candy Brand)

Makes 1 large or 2 small cheese balls

2 (8 oz.) cream cheese, not softened
¼ cup green pepper, chopped
¼ cup green onion, chopped
1 Tbsp. "Crazy Jane's Mixed Up Seasoning" packet (you can find at most grocery stores)
Pecans or walnuts, chopped

Mix all except nuts with hands. Roll in nuts. Chill.

CRESCENT COVERED BRIE ROLL
(Jamie Miller)

Serves 6

1 (8 oz.) can Pillsbury refrigerated crescent dinner rolls
1 round (8 oz.) Brie cheese
1 egg, beaten

Unroll dough; separate crosswise in 2 sections. Press to seal perforations, forming 2 squares. On cookie sheet, place cheese in center of 1 dough square. Cover with remaining square of cheese. Press dough evenly around the cheese and fold bottom edges over top edges. Press to seal completely. Brush with beaten egg. Bake 20-24 minutes at 350° or until golden brown. Serve as is, or with crackers or chips.

AMAZING CHEESE TORTE APPETIZER
(Laurette Walton)

Serves 8-10

10 oz. sharp cheddar cheese

1 cup pecans

1 bunch green onions finely chopped

2 (8 oz.) packages of softened cream cheese

⅓ cup chutney

⅓ cup frozen chopped spinach (thawed, drained, and blotted dry)

¼ tsp. garlic salt

1st layer:
Combine cheese, pecans and onions. Place ½ of mixture in deep dish or soufflé bowl.

2nd layer:
Combine 1 package cream cheese with chutney and blend and spread over cheese.

3rd layer:
Blend 1 package cream cheese, spinach, and garlic salt. Spread over chutney layer.

4th layer:
Top with remaining cheddar cheese mixture. Chill. Serve with crackers.

HAM AND CHEESE ROUND
(Tina Cole)

Serves 8-10

1 large "Brown and Serve" French round
1 med. yellow onion, finely chopped
3 Tbsp. sesame or poppy seeds
1 cup butter
1 lb. ham very thinly sliced
1 lb. Swiss cheese very thinly sliced
4 strips bacon, uncooked
Toothpicks

Slice unbaked bread in 1 inch strips almost completely through to bottom crust. Sauté onions and seeds in ¾ cup butter until transparent. Spoon butter/onion in between slices as you spread them open with fingers. Working from the center slice, stuff ham between the slices, repeat with cheese. (Slices are very full.) Melt remaining ¼ cup of butter and brush over the top of bread. Squeeze loaf together and lay bacon over loaf like straps, securing with toothpicks. Place loaf on sprayed cookie sheet, and bake uncovered according to bread wrapper directions, approx. 15-20 minutes (bacon will be crisp.) Place on tray and slice all the way through in 1 inch slices, perpendicular to original slices, making a grid. Pull out squares.

Cathy & Tina in their dressing room just prior to performing with The Four King Cousins in Las Vegas 1969

CRAB PUFFS
(Donna King Conkling)

Makes 2 dozen

1 package frozen wonton squares, thawed
Peanut oil
1 (7oz.) can crab meat
2 drops sesame oil
8 oz. cream cheese
2 Tbsp. soft bread crumbs

Heat 1" peanut oil in skillet until very hot (375°.) Mix all ingredients and place 1 tsp. of mixture in the center of each wonton. Fold the corners to the center, one at a time; moisten and seal the edges. Drop into oil for 3 minutes, turning ½ way, until slightly brown. Drain. Serve with Chinese mustard.

BROILED CRAB AND CHEESE SANDWICHES
(Carolyn Cameron)

Makes enough to top 8 English Muffin halves

1 can or 1 cup fresh crab
½ tsp. Worcestershire sauce
½ cup grated cheddar cheese
2 Tbsp. chopped green onion
Just enough mayonnaise to moisten
Lawry's to taste
½ tsp. mustard
4 English muffins

Add everything, a little at a time, to the crab. You may want to adjust the amounts to your taste. Pile high on English muffins and stick under the broiler until hot and bubbly.

TORTILLA ROLL-UPS
(Erin Arnett)

Makes 2 dozen tortillas to cut into 1" appetizers

8 oz. cream cheese
16 oz. sour cream
2 bunches of green onions
3 (7 oz.) cans chopped green chilies
2 dozen flour tortillas
Grated cheese (optional)
Bacon bits (optional)
Lawry's to taste
Garlic salt to taste

Blend all ingredients together in a large bowl until smooth. Spread over individual tortillas and roll each tortilla up into a cylinder shape. Refrigerate for an hour (you might need to put a toothpick in it to hold its shape or I put the cylinders back in the tortilla bag altogether to hold their shape.) Cut each into 1 inch pieces and serve.

WORLD'S EASIEST AND BEST APPETIZER
(Donna King Conkling)

Serves 8

1 box crackers or 1 bag tortilla chips
8 oz. cream cheese, not softened

Possible toppings:
1 jar salsa or
1 jar cocktail sauce and fresh baby shrimp or
1 jar mint jelly

Arrange crackers or chips on tray. Choose 1 of the toppings to spoon over the cream cheese. Each choice offers a completely different flavor. So easy but it will all be eaten!

SPICED PARTY PECANS
(Wendy Moran)

Be careful not to eat them all in one sitting!

Makes 6 cups

2 Tbsp. Butter, melted
½ tsp. Tabasco sauce
2 Tbsp. Molasses
1 ½ cups sugar
2 tsp. cinnamon
½ tsp. nutmeg

1 egg white
1 Tbsp. Vanilla
6 cups pecans
1 tsp. salt
1 tsp. ginger

Mix the items in the first column together until well combined. Set aside. In a large bowl, whisk the egg and vanilla until frothy. Add nuts and toss and coat. Add spice mixture and mix well. Spread nuts on a greased baking sheet. Bake at 250° for 45 min. (Stir nuts and remix half-way through baking.)

SHRIMP MOLD
(Cathy Green)

Serves 8

8oz. cream cheese
1 can cream of mushroom soup
6 green onions, chopped
1 can water chestnuts, chopped

¾ cup mayonnaise
1 ½ pkgs. unflavored gelatin
2 cans shrimp (tiny)

Mix cream cheese, mayo, soup, and gelatin in glass bowl. Microwave until warm, approximately 1 minute. Mix well, add the rest. Spray Pam on a mold (A fish mold is great.) Refrigerate overnight. Serve with crackers.

Breads

"The King Family Show" 1969

BRUSCHETTA
(Diana Driggs)

Makes 1 cup of topping

4 large ripe tomatoes (cored and diced)
2 Tbsp. fresh basil
1 Tbsp. Italian parsley
3 tsp. white wine vinegar
2 Tbsp. extra virgin olive oil
Garlic salt and pepper to taste
Italian bread

Mix all together. Serve on loaf of crusty Italian Bread.

LEMON BREAD
(Amy Nottingham)

Makes 1 loaf

1 cup sugar
2 eggs
½ cup melted butter
½ cup milk
1 ½ cups flour

1 tsp. baking powder
Dash of salt
Zest of 1 ½ lemons
⅓ cup powdered sugar
Juice on 1 lemon

Mix all ingredients. Grease a 5x9 loaf pan, pour mixture into pan and bake 45-60 minutes at 350°.

Glaze: Mix together powdered sugar and lemon juice. Pour over loaf when still hot. Let cool before serving.

WORLD'S BEST BANANA BREAD
(Tina Cole)

Tina got this recipe from her MY THREE SONS TV mother-in-law-turned-real-life-mother-in-law, Beverly Garland, and hasn't thrown out an over-ripe banana since. It's so easy to make, it's one of the first recipes her daughters, Chelsea and Sammi, made when they were in middle-school.

Makes 2 loaves

6 ripe bananas - mashed (approx. 3 cups)
2 ¾ cup cake flour   4 eggs, well beaten
2 tsp. baking soda   2 Tbsp. sour cream
1 tsp. salt   Juice of 1 lemon
1 cup butter, softened   2 cups sugar

Lightly grease 2 loaf pans 5x9". Sift dry Ingredients together (except sugar) 3 times and set aside. With electric beaters, cream butter and sugar until light and fluffy. Add mashed bananas and beat well. Add eggs and mix well. Blend sifted dry ingredients into banana mixture; do not over-mix. Stir in sour cream and lemon juice. Pour mixture into prepared pans and bake at 350° for 45 min-1 hour, until firm in center and edges begin to pull away from pans. Cool 10 minutes before removing from pans.

Cathy & Tina in 1972

FRIED SCONES
(Tina Cole)

So easy. And unlike most scones, these are light and airy, and I defy you to stop at only one!

Makes 3-4 dozen

3 Tbsp. yeast	5 cups flour
4 cups warm water	1 Tbsp. salt
4 Tbsp. sugar	4 more cups flour
3 Tbsp. oil	

In bowl sprinkle yeast over warm water. Sprinkle sugar over yeast; let sit 5 minutes. Stir in oil. Stir in 5 cups of flour, 1 cup at a time. Mix together salt and 4 remaining cups of flour and stir into mixture, 1 cup at a time. Oil hands and form dough into a ball and then put in bowl and cover with a towel. Let stand 30 minutes in a warm, draft free place to rise. Oil hands and punch down. Turn out ¼ of dough on greased board and pat or roll out. With pizza cutter, cut in squares 2" or larger. Fry in hot oil until puffed and golden. (I like to use an electric fryer.) Drain. Roll lightly in sugar or dust with powdered sugar. Serve hot with butter, jams, jellies, applesauce, honey, apple butter, etc.

Tina, Vonnie & Cathy in 2009

BISCUIT SCONES
(Phyllis Heim)

Makes 8 triangles

4 cups self-rising flour
1 can regular Sprite
1 cup heavy cream
½ tsp. salt

Mix all ingredients and handle lightly. Work with pastry knife if possible and turn out on floured board. Continue to handle lightly, kneading slightly. Shape into a round and cut into triangles like pizza slices. Bake at 400° for about 20 minutes.

PUMPKIN BISCUITS
(Xan Albright)

Makes 12-15 biscuits

2 cups Bisquick
2 tsp. sugar
1 ½ tsp. pumpkin pie spice
⅔ cups canned pumpkin
2 tsp. milk

Mix all to form soft dough. Beat 30 seconds. Turn dough onto dusted surface. Roll and shape into ball. Knead 10 times. Roll out ½" thick and cut with round cutter. Bake on an ungreased sheet at 450° for 12 minutes. Serve with Spiced Honey Spread.

Spiced Honey Spread: (Mix all together & serve with hot biscuits)
½ cup butter, softened
¼ tsp. pumpkin pie spice
2 tsp. honey

GERMAN PUMPKIN BREAD
(Phyllis Heim)

Makes 4 loaves

3 ½ cups flour	3 cups sugar
1 tsp. baking soda	½ tsp. nutmeg
1 ½ tsp. cinnamon	1 tsp. salt
4 eggs	¾ cup water
1 cup oil	1 cup walnuts
1 cup raisins	2 cups canned pumpkin

Mix well and spray pans with Pam. Baking time varies according to size of pan. Recipe makes three large (8" x 3 5/8") plus one small (5 ¾" x 3 ¼") loaves. Sift dry ingredients together and make a well in the center. Add remaining ingredients. Bake small loaf 45 minutes, large loaves 55 minutes at 350°.

PUMPKIN CHOCOLATE CHIP MUFFINS
(Laurette Walton)

Makes 10-12 muffins

1 ⅔ cups flour	¼ tsp. salt
1 cup sugar	2 eggs
1 tsp. pumpkin pie spice	1 cup canned pumpkin
1 tsp. cinnamon	½ cup melted butter
1 tsp. baking soda	1 cup mini chocolate chips
¼ tsp. baking powder	

Mix all dry ingredients. Beat eggs, pumpkin and butter and add to dry ingredients. Stir in chips. Bake in regular or mini muffin tins at 350° for 20-25 minutes.

TINA'S 6 WEEK "BLAST-OUT" BRAN MUFFINS
(Tina Cole)

Batter stores in fridge for up to 6 weeks

Makes 3 dozen

2 cups Kellogg's All Bran Cereal (long fibers)
2 cups sugar
4 cups 100% Bran (nuggets or buds)
1 cup brown sugar
1 ½ cups butter, softened
4 eggs, beaten
2 cups boiling water
1 cup raisins
5 tsp. baking soda
1 quart buttermilk
1 cup ea. walnuts or pecans
5 tsp. salt
5 cups flour

Put "All Bran" fibers in small bowl, pour boiling water over fibers, and mix – let sit 5 min. In large bowl, cream butter and sugar until fluffy. Add beaten eggs one at a time and mix. Blend in buttermilk. Stir in softened "All Bran" fibers and water, mixing well. Sift flour, salt, and baking soda and add to mixture, stirring only until just blended. DO NOT over-mix. Stir in remaining ingredients (nuts which are optional, should be chopped) and bake OR store in air-tight container in fridge for up to 6 weeks, using when desired. DO NOT MIX ONCE IT HAS BEEN STORED. To bake – scoop batter into greased muffin cups, filled ⅔ full. Bake 400° for 15-20 min.

CAROLYN'S DINNER ROLLS
(Carolyn Cameron)
Perfect for holidays or any occasion

Makes 40 rolls
2 packages yeast
½ cup warm water mixed with
    2 Tbsp. sugar of the ½ cup sugar listed below.

Put yeast packages in warm water/sugar. Stir and set aside.

½ c. milk	½ cup sugar
1 ½ cubes butter, melted	¼ cup additional butter
2 eggs	6-7 cups flour
2 tsp. salt	

Heat milk and ¼ cup butter, but do not boil. Combine remaining ingredients in a large bowl and add the hot milk. Mix well, but you really do not have to knead it. I have a bread mixer which makes it easier but you can do it by hand. Put in buttered bowl covered with a slightly wet cloth, and let rise in oven for 2 hours. (Hint: I turn my oven on to 200° and then turn it off immediately. If your kitchen is warm, you can just leave bowl on the counter. The warmth of the oven helps it to rise). After it has risen, punch down and pinch off dough to make small 1 ½-2 inch balls in size. Roll balls in melted butter and place in 9x13 pan, not touching, about 1 inch apart. Let rise 1 hour, or until they are touching and really puffy. Bake in a 375° oven for 20 minutes. These freeze really well when they are hot right out of the oven.

FOCACCIA
(Diana Driggs)

Serves 9

1 onion, finely chopped	1 tsp. baking powder
2 beaten eggs	1 tsp. salt
Oregano and basil to taste	4 Tbsp. oil
Salt and pepper to taste	1 ½ cups milk
3 cups flour	1 cup Parmesan cheese

Lightly brown the chopped onion in oil. Once the onions are brown, add the beaten eggs, oregano, basil, salt and pepper to taste. Set aside. Mix flour, baking powder and salt in a large mixing bowl. Add oil and milk to obtain a doughy consistency. With wet hands, spread dough evenly in a greased 9x13 pan. Spread onion/egg mixture evenly over dough. Sprinkle the Parmesan cheese lightly to cover the top. Optional – add Mozzarella cheese the last few minutes of cooking. Bake at 350° for 25 min.

THE PERFECT BLUEBERRY MUFFIN
(Sarah Thomas)

Makes 12 muffins

2 cups flour	1 cup milk
½ cup sugar	1 egg
1 Tbsp. baking powder	¼ cup oil
1 tsp. salt	2 cups blueberries

Mix all together, stirring in blueberries last. Bake at 400° for 22-25 minutes (until tops are light brown.)

TORTA FRITA
(Diana Driggs)

Growing up in Uruguay I remember rainy days were the time to make Torta Fritas. We've kept that tradition in our home and we know that if it rains all night, the kids will wake us up earlier than usual and ask for Tortas Fritas. Now they can help make it and we all enjoy it any time of the day.

1 Tbsp. butter	1 cup milk
1 tsp. salt	3-4 cups of flour
1 tsp. baking powder	Oil

Melt butter with the milk, add salt. Let it cool off a little bit. Mix flour and baking soda in a medium size bowl and add the milk mixture, stir well. Make soft dough, not sticky. Divide the dough into balls of about 1 ½ to 2 inches in diameter. Roll each ball on a floured board until you have a circle of about 6 inches in diameter. Make a hole in the middle with your finger and fry with oil. You need enough oil to cover it. As soon as it turns a light, golden color, turn it over and cook on other side. Place on a paper towel-lined dish to dry. Top with powdered sugar, honey or jam. Or just eat it plain. Great with hot chocolate!

The King Family and the world's longest hot dog

SPOON BREAD (CORNBREAD)
(Liza Rey)

Liza has become quite famous in her community for this recipe. Her two sons (who are world-famous for their Grammy-nominated Indie rock band "Arcade Fire") always request this yummy bread when they return home from their concert tours.

Serves 6

1 can creamed corn	1 tsp. baking soda
¾ cup milk	2 eggs, slightly beaten
1 cup cornmeal	1 (4 oz.) can green chilies, chopped
1 tsp. salt	1-2 cups grated cheddar cheese

Mix everything except the chilies and cheese. Spread ½ of the mixture into a greased 9" pan. Spread the chilies and ½ the grated cheese over this. Pour the remaining batter over and cover with more grated cheese. Bake for 40 minutes at 400°. Serve with soup or chili.

CORN PUDDING
(Carolyn Cameron, Shauna Elliott)

Serves 9

6 ears fresh corn	6 eggs
8 oz. cream cheese softened	¾ cup butter
1 Tbsp. baking powder	Pinch of salt

Remove all the corn from the ears. Run a spoon down the sides of each ear to remove pulp and to get all the juice. Beat the eggs and combine with all the ingredients. Bake in 8x8 pan at 300° for 40-50 min.

MAURI BREAD
(Amy Nottingham)

Makes 3 loaves

1 cup flour
4 cups water
1 cup sugar
2 Tbsp. yeast
9 cups flour

Mix 1st four ingredients and let rest 10 minutes. Add the remaining flour; knead. Let rise 20 minutes. Divide into 3 loaves, place all 3 into a 9x13 pan. Let rise 30 minutes. Bake 40 minutes at 350°.

HOT GOOEY CHEESE BREAD
(Laurette Walton)

Serves 8

1 loaf French, Vienna or Italian bread
1 tsp. (or more of course) Lawry's
8-16 oz. Swiss cheese, grated   ½ tsp. lemon juice
1 cup butter   1 Tbsp. dry mustard
2 Tbsp. dried onion   2 Tbsp. poppy seeds

Slice loaf in criss-cross pattern leaving ½-1" uncut at bottom. Melt butter. Add onion, Lawry's, lemon juice, mustard and stir well. Place Swiss cheese between wedges of bread then sprinkle with poppy seeds. Pour the butter mixture over the bread making sure to spread evenly. Wrap tightly in foil and bake at 350° for at least 30 min. Pull back foil and simply pull apart and enjoy. You'll eat the whole loaf!

CHEESE PUFF GOUGÈRE
(Tina Cole)

Gougère is a breeze-of-a-method for making pastry that originated many, many years ago in France. Much like a glorified cream puff or pop-over, it is a beautiful substitute for bread with soups, stews, or salads.

Serves 6-8
1 cup milk
¼ cup butter, cut into pieces
½ tsp. salt
Dash of pepper
1 cup flour, unsifted
4 eggs
1 cup Swiss cheese, shredded and divided

In heavy, 2-quart saucepan, heat milk, butter, salt and pepper, bringing to a full boil. Add the flour all at once, stirring constantly. Almost immediately the dough will leave the sides of the pan and form a ball. Remove from heat. With the spoon beat the eggs into the dough, one at a time, until the mixture is smooth and well blended. Stir in ½ of cheese - dough will be very sticky. Using ¾ of the dough, place 8 spoonfuls in a circle on an ungreased baking sheet. The mounds should barely touch each other, forming a circle about 8 inches in diameter with a 2-inch space in the center. With the rest of the dough, place a smaller mound on the top of each larger one. Sprinkle remaining ½ cup of cheese over all. Bake at 375° for 45 min. or until puffs are lightly browned and crisp. Do not open oven door for the first 40 min. of baking. Serve immediately.

The King Kids performing on the 1968 TV special
"Valentine's Day with the King Family"

RECIPE INDEX

MAIN DISHES
ALVINO'S GREEK LEG OF LAMB, 28
APPLE CURRY CHICKEN, 36
BARBEQUE BEEF FOR SANDWICHES, 16
BARBEQUE BEEF FOR PORK ALTERNATE, 17
BARBECUED CHICKEN PIZZA, 32
BARBECUED PORK RIBS, 29
BEEFY BEAN BAKE, 27
BERRIED PORK TENDERLOIN, 31
CAJUN CHICKEN, 38
CATHY'S PASTA BROCCOLI W/ TURKEY, 33
CHEESE & SPINACH FILLED MANICOTTI, 56
CHICK'S CHILI RELLENOS, 62-63
CHICKEN À LA KING, 35-36
CHICKEN CACCIATORI, 52
CHICKEN CHOW MEIN, 47
CHICKEN DIVAN, 42
CHICKEN MANDARIN, 39
CHICKEN TETTRAZINI, 51
CHICKEN W/ PEPPERS & SHERRY, 40
CHILI & BEANS, 63
CONKLING CHICKEN CRESCENT ROLL-UPS, 41-42
CRANBERRY CHICKEN, 43
CROCKPOT LASAGNA, 54
CROCKPOT TACO CASSEROLE, 60
DALE'S BBQ SHRIMP CREOLE, 71
DONNA BELLA À LA FARFELLA, 55
DRIGGSUS STEAK SEASONING, 15
ENCHILADAS VERDES, 61
EXOTIC CHICKEN, 44
FAJITAS, 59
FRESH BARBECUED TROUT, 69
FLANK STEAK MARINADE, 25
HAM SOUFFLÉ, 67
HOT CHICKEN SALAD, 34
ITALIAN SURPRISE, 52
KOREAN STEAK SKEWERS, 26
LEFTOVER HAM CSSEROLE, 67
LEMON MUSTARD MARINADE FOR CHICHEN, 50
MEXICAN CHICKEN CASSEROLE, 57
MEXICAN LASAGNA, 60
OLD WORLD LASAGNA, 53
PAELLA, 70
PESTO PIZZA, 50
POACHED SALMON, 68
POPPY SEED CHICKEN, 45
PORK CHOPS W/APPLES, 31
PSEUDO CHICKEN CORDON BLEU, 45
PSEUDO ROTISSERIE CHICKEN, 49
PULLED SWEET PORK, 30
ROCKY MOUNTAIN RIBS, 32
SAUSAGE CASSEROLE, 64
SPICY GARLIC PRIME RIB EYE, 24
SPINACH FETA PIE, 60
ST. PATRICK'S CORN BEEF/CABBAGE, 65
SWEDISH MEATBALLS, 26
SWEET MEATLOAF, 25
TARRAGON CHICKEN, 34-35
TINA'S BEEF STROGANOFF, 14
TINA'S PILGRIM'S PIE, 22-24
TINA'S SHEPHERD'S PIE, 18-21
TUSCANY CHICKEN, 48
TWICE BAKED POTATOES W/ HAM, 66
WHITE CHICKEN CHILI, 46
WILSON SISTER'S ITALIAN CHICKEN, 43

SOUPS
BROCCOLI CHEESE SOUP, 78
CHEESY HAM CHOWDER, 80
CREAM OF CHICKEN SOUP, 77
GREEK LEMON RICE SOUP, 81
MINESTRONE SOUP, 79
NAVY BEAN SOUP, 75
POTATO CHICKEN POTAGE, 74
SANTA ANA ALBONDIGAS SOUP, 83
TINA'S NORWEGIAN CAULIFLOWER SOUP, 82
TOMATO CLAM BISQUE, 75
TORTELLINI SOUP, 81
TORTILLA SOUP CROCKPOT, 76

SALADS & DRESSINGS
ARUGULA ORZO SALAD, 98
ASPARAGUS POTATO SALAD, 107
BOW TIE CHICKEN SALAD, 96
BROCCOLI SALAD, 90
CHICKEN PASTA PRIMAVERA, 108
CHICKEN SALAD, 97
CHINESE CABBAGE SALAD, 98
CHINESE CHICKEN SALAD, 97
CREAMY CUCUMBER/TOMATO SALAD, 105
DONNA'S POTATO SALAD, 86-87
FETA SALAD, 89
FROZEN FRUIT SALAD, 95
HOLIDAY JELL-O SALAD, 91
KING FAMILY MANDARIN ORANGE SALAD, 104-105
ONLY TRUE BLUE CHEESE DRESSING, 102
ORANGE - GRAPEFRUIT SALAD, 93
PASTA SALAD ORIENTAL, 99
PEACH/GRAPE SALAD, 90
PEAR LIME JELL-O, 90
RASPBERRY/BLUEBERRY SALAD, 88

RASPBERRY/VEGGIE SALAD MOLD, 106
RICE AND SHRIMP SALAD, 106
SANTA ROSA VALLEY SALAD, 103
SPINACH CRAISIN SALAD, 92-93
STEAK SUPPER SALAD, 94
STRAWBERRY SPINACH SALAD, 101
SUMMER SALAD, 109
VEGETABLE SALAD, 89
WENDY'S FRESH SALAD, 110
WINTER SALAD W/ PEARS, 100

BRUNCHES & VEGETABLES
AEBLESKIVERS, 121
BAKED FRUIT, 132
CANDIED SWEET POTATOES & APPLES, 131
CARROT SOUFFLÉ, 128
CHILI EGG PUFF, 117
CREAMED CORN, 126
CREAMED POTATOES AND PEAS, 129
FRESH GREEN BEANS, 126
GLAZED CARROTS À LA DONNA, 124
KING SISTERS '50s LUNCHEON LOAF, 114
OATMEAL PANCAKES, 120
PICNIC BAKED BEANS, 127
POTATOES O'BRIEN, 130
POTATOES OLIVER, 130
PUMPKIN PANCAKES, 118
SPACK MORTENSEN'S DILL PICKLES, 133
SPICED APPLES, 115
SQUASH CASSEROLE, 124
STUFFED FRENCH TOAST, 121
TAHOE BRUNCH, 123
TINA'S GERMAN PANCAKES, 119
TUNA RITZ SANDWICHES, 122
VONNIE'S SCRAMBLED EGGS, 117
VONNIES CHRISTMAS SNAUSAGES, 116
YUMMY CORN, 125
ZUCCHINI CASSEROLE, 125

DESSERTS
5 MINUTE CHOCOLATE MUG CAKE, 160-161
ANGEL SUGAR COOKIES, 191
AUNT LILLY'S MAYONNAISE CAKE, 141-143
BANANA CAKE WITH QUICK CARAMEL FROSTING, 144-145
BLUEBERRY CREAM PIE, 174
BROWNIE CHEESECAKE, 168
CARMELITAS, 193
CHICK'S CHEESECAKE, 169
CHOCOLATE ANGEL FOOD CAKE, 145
CHOCOLATE CHIP PUDDING COOKIES, 190
CHOCOLATE FONDUE, 136
CHOCOLATE MINT COOKIES, 185
CHOCOLATE MOUSSE PIE, 167
CHOCOLATE ORANGE PIE, 165
CHOCOLATE PISTACHIO CAKE, 158-159
CHOCOLATE SILK PIE, 166
CHOCOLATE TORTE, 161
CHOCOLATE VELVET CREAM CAKE, 151
COCONUT CRUNCH CHOCOLATE CHIP COOKIES, 193
COMPANY CAKE, 143
CRANK KIDS BIRTHDAT FUNNEL CAKE, 162
CROCKPOT CHOCOLATE CHIP PUDDING CAKE, 156
CUSTARD DESSERT, 177
DELUXE LEMON BARS, 189
DERBY PIE, 171
DEVILISH CHOCOLATE CAKE, 146
DONNA & CAROLYN'S CHERRY CREAM PIE, 174
DONNA'S HOT FUDGE SAUCE, 136
ENGLISH TOFFEE, 196
FRENCH HOT CHOCOLATE ICE CREAM PIE, 167
FRENCH MINT PIE, 177
FUDGE-TOPPED BROWNIES, 182
GINGERBREAD WITH WARM LEMON SAUCE, 147
GREAT CARROT CAKE, 150
HOMEMADE FRUIT ICE CREAM, 178
HOMEMADE CHOCOLATE ICE CREAM, 181
RICHIE KING CLARKE'S HOMEMADE VANILLA ICE CREAM, 180
HOMEMADE VANILLA PUDDING ICE CREAM, 179
KEY LIME PIE, 172
LEMON ANGEL PIE, 173
LEMON DROP COOKIES, 184
LEMON-PLUM TOUR CAKE, 154-155
MAGIC COOKIE BARS, 189
MICROWAVE PEANUT BRITTLE, 197
MILK CHOCO BUTTERSCOTCH CAFÉ, 187
MISSISSIPPI MUD CAKE, 157
MUDDIE BUDDIES, 198
NO BAKE PEANUTTY/CHOC DROPS, 186
OATMEAL SCOTCHIES, 183
PEACH CARAMEL CHEESECAKE, 170-171
PEACH COBBLER, 164
PEANUT BUTTER BLOSSOM COOKIES, 187
PEANUT BUTTER CREAM PIE, 173
PEAR PIE, 175
PEARL'S DIVINITY, 194-195
PIONEER APPLESAUCE DESSERT, 138
PUMPKIN BARS, 188
PUMPKIN CAKE, 152
PUMPKIN CHIFFON PIE, 176
PUMPKIN SURPRISE, 139
RAW APPLE CAKE, 149
SELF FILLED CUPCAKES, 159

SHERBET AND FRUIT MOUND, 178
SOUR CREAM POPPY SEED CAKE, 153
STEVO'S LEMONADE ICE CREAM PIE, 163
STRAWBERRY CAKE WITH STRAWBERRY
          CREAM CHEESE FROSTING, 148-149
TINA'S SINFULLY DELICIOUS
          FAGAGA HOT FUDGE, 137
TRIFLE CHRISTMAS PUDDING, 140
ULTIMATE SUGAR COOKIE, 190
VONNIE'S PIE CRUST, 163
WHITE CHOCOLATE CRUNCH, 195
YUMMY SHORTBREAD COOKIES W/JAM, 192
YUMMY SQUARES, 186

BEVERAGES, DIPS, SAUCES, & APPETIZERS
AMAZING CHEESE TORTE, 215
BAKED BEAN DIP, 209
BARBEQUE SAUCE, 212
BEST GUACAMOLE SAUCE IN TOWN, 206
BLENDER BÉARNAISE, 210
BLENDER HOLLANDAISE, 210
BLUE CHEESE BALLS, 213
BROILED CRAB & CHEESE SANDWICHES, 217
CINNAMON SCENTED
          CRANAPPLE SAUCE, 211
CRAB PUFFS, 217
CRESCENT COVERED BRIE ROLL, 214
FRESH FRUIT LEMONADE, 205
FROSTY, ZESTYPARTY PUNCH, 204
FRUIT DIP, 206
GOURMET HOT CHOCOLATE, 203
GREG'S SALSA, 208
HAM AND CHEESE ROUND, 216

HOT ARTICHOKE DIP, 207
HOT HOLIDAY CIDER, 202-203
JIM CONKLING'S FAMOUS EGG NOG, 202
LIME CUCUMBER PUNCH, 205
MAXINE'S BEST PUNCH EVER, 204
MIXED UP CHEESE BALL, 214
ROB'S GUACAMOLE, 208
ROSE'S SAUCE, 212
SHRIMP MOLD, 219
SPICED PARTY PECANS, 219
TORTILLA ROLL-UPS, 218
WORLD'S EASIEST/BEST APPETIZER, 218

BREADS
BISCUIT SCONES, 225
BLUEBERRY MUFFIN, 229
BRUSCHETA, 222
CAROLYN'S DINNER ROLLS, 228
CHEESE PUFF GOUGERE, 233
CORN PUDDING, 231
FOCACCIA, 229
FRIED SCONES, 224
GERMAN PUMPKIN BREAD, 226
HOT GOOEY CHEESE BREAD, 232
LEMON BREAD, 222
MAURI BREAD, 222
PUMPKIN BISCUITS, 225
PUMPKIN CHOCOLATE CHIP MUFFINS, 266
SPOON BREAD (CORNBREAD), 231
TINA'S BLAST-OUT BRAN MUFFINS, 227
TORTA FRITA, 230
WORLD'S BEST BANANA BREAD, 223

The Driggs Family of Entertainers - the original family band in the early 1930s. (Grandpa William King Driggs, Alyce, Luise, Karleton, Maxine, Grandma Pearl Driggs, Bill, Donna & Vonnie)

ALSO AVAILABLE FROM the

5 Classic Albums on CD for the first time!

CHRISTMAS WITH THE KING FAMILY
(soundtrack highlights from the new Public TV special, includes original 1965 album and 11 bonus tracks from the King Family's Christmas TV specials) **CCM-2071**

**THE KING FAMILY LIVE! IN THE ROUND &
THE NEW SOUNDS OF THE FABULOUS KING SISTERS**
(2 albums on 1 CD) **CCM-2072**

THE KING FAMILY SHOW! & THE KING FAMILY ALBUM
(2 albums on 1 CD - includes 2 bonus tracks by The King Cousins) **CCM-2073**

New Holiday Special On DVD!

AS SEEN ON PUBLIC TELEVISION!
CHRISTMAS WITH THE KING FAMILY is a song filled celebration of the King Family's legendary Christmas TV specials! Features a wealth of classic clips in addition to contemporary interviews with Yvonne & Marilyn King, Tina Cole, Cathy (Cole) Green, Cam Clarke, Ric de Azevedo and cousins Xan, Candy, Jamie, Laurette and Susannah! **BONUS MATERIAL** includes the entire 1967 King Family Christmas special - first time on DVD!
IEG2175

WWW.OFFICIALKINGFAMILY.COM

Bear Manor Media

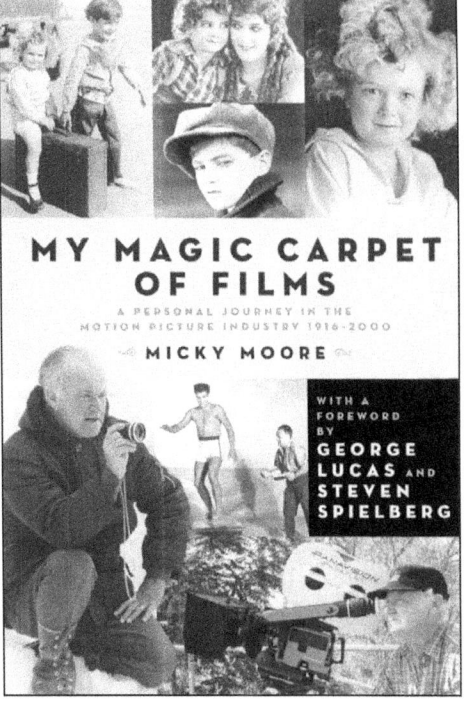
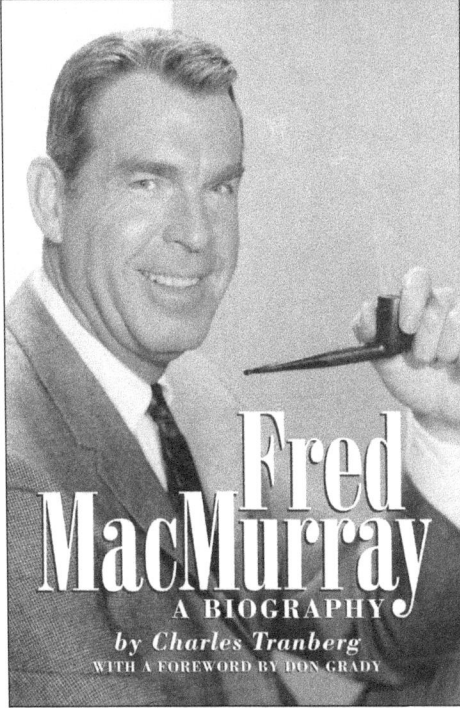

Classic Cinema.
Timeless TV.
Retro Radio.

WWW.BEARMANORMEDIA.COM

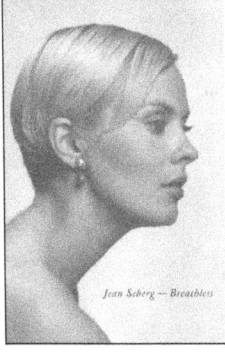

www.ingramcontent.com/pod-product-compliance
Lightning Source LLC
Chambersburg PA
CBHW062015220426
43662CB00010B/1336